# LIVERPOOL 1995

# LIVERPOOL 1995

CREATED BY GREG PERCIVAL
AND HUGH GOLLNER
EDITORIAL BY KEN ROGERS

OXFORD • INTERNATIONAL • PUBLICATIONS

LIVERPOOL
LIVERPOOL
Coca-Cola

# GLORY RETURNS TO ANFIELD

SIR STANLEY MATTHEWS was one of the most skillful forwards the English game has ever seen. Back in the Fifties, he was dubbed the 'Wizard of the Wing' by adoring fans. In 1953, the great man graced Wembley Stadium with a stunning display of sorcery to help Blackpool win the FA Cup. The Matthews Final is part and parcel of soccer folklore.

With Sir Stanley as the chief guest of honour at the Coca-Cola Cup Final on 2 April, perhaps it was written in the stars that another winger with grace and style would dance down the touchline and thrill a capacity crowd with his skill, verve and youthfulness.

Steve McManaman is very much the modern version of Matthews. In many respects that is the ultimate tribute. But it is a compliment that is well deserved.

If the 1994/95 campaign goes down in history as the year of the great Reds revival, it will also go down as the period in which a young Merseysider showed a real desire to entertain the nation at every twist and turn. Certainly, no one could deny McManaman his moment of personal glory as he inspired a 2-1 Liverpool victory over Bolton to help manager, Roy Evans, claim the Coca-Cola Cup in his first full season in charge.

The victory would come towards the end of a long and eventful campaign. That it takes its place at the start of this record of a tremendous year emphasises its importance to the Reds. Not only did it signal that the club was back in business, it also secured European action for a club that was for a decade the major force in European soccer.

The other Euro giants would immediately take note that a famous name was back in the frame. Yes, Wembley 1995 was something very special for the men from Anfield.

Up in the Royal Box, ready to hand over the trophy, a certain Mr Matthews gave a knowing smile. He was clearly delighted that a side had triumphed, showing teamwork and star quality – but most of all skill. Two goal hero McManaman was the young man who had set the standards for the rest to follow.

This was the fifth time the Reds had won this particular competition, in all of its various guises. None of their previous victories were as sweet, simply because it had been three years – a long time at Anfield – since a piece of silverware had resided in the most famous trophy room in the land.

Liverpool went out from the first whistle and stamped their authority on the game. Robbie Fowler forced 'keeper, Keith Branagan, in to making a low save after 13 minutes. Ian Rush then blazed over following a surging left wing run by McManaman. But the Reds would not have it all their own way. Alan Thompson struck a dipping shot that was heading into the top corner until David James flew to his left to touch it onto the bar.

Enter McManaman to stun Bolton with a brilliant opener. John Barnes set up the move midway inside the Bolton half. McManaman set off on a mazy run that took him past Alan Stubbs and Scott Green before he placed a low shot into the far corner of Branagan's goal.

Wanderers were down, but they were not out. They began the second period with much more verve and Mixu Paatelainen and Alan Thompson had the Merseyside fans holding their breath.

McManaman now gave Bolton something to think about when he fired a shot over the top. It helped to give the Reds more momentum, and the young winger now demonstrated his genuine star quality with a delightful second goal. He weaved into the box and curled a right foot effort into the far corner of the net with Branagan well beaten.

But First Division Bolton refused to give up the chase. Thompson cracked home an excellent effort after 69 minutes to give his side a lifeline. But Liverpool would not be denied.

The smiles on the faces of the players as they climbed the steps of the Royal Box to receive the trophy was matched only by the sheer delight on the face of manager Evans. So elated was he with the success that he slept with the trophy in his hotel bedroom.

He rose from his slumber to say: *"When I walked off the pitch yesterday, I realised just what a responsibility I have as manager. Seeing so many happy people meant so much to me. You always want to win games, but I realised just how much the Liverpool fans wanted us to win this trophy.*

*"I wanted it to be a friendly final and it turned out that way. I thought our fans were different class. They were magnificent with the Bolton supporters. Coca-Cola helped make the atmosphere special and I don't think it will be bettered at Wembley for a long time."*

On his team, the proud manager said: *"I've never seen so many players so delighted to win something. This situation is new to some of our lads. The bus journey back to the hotel after the game was unbelievable. All the players really enjoyed it.*

*"I wanted them to feel like winners and they do now. Now we all want more of it."*

Bolton had been stern opponents. They emphasised their battling qualities the following month by securing a return to soccer's top flight in the promotion play-offs. Wanderers' success on the League front heightened Liverpool's pleasure at winning at Wembley.

For their part, the Reds took the greatest satisfaction of all from having secured that automatic place in the UEFA Cup, a trophy that had resided at Anfield in 1972-73 and 1975-76.

In 1984, when the Merseysiders won the Champions Cup for the forth time, Liverpool were the undisputed kings of Europe. Now this Coca-Cola Cup triumph had put the men from Anfield back on the continental glory trail.

Half of the city of Liverpool travelled to Wembley Stadium on 2 April for the Coca-Cola Cup Final against Bolton Wanderers. A tremendous roar greeted the players as they stepped in to the Spring sunshine for their biggest game of the season. The flags and banners were raised aloft by the fans in a fitting salute to their Anfield heroes.

The players respond by waving to the crowd and picking out familiar faces *(right)*. Then the Cup Final squad is introduced to Sir Stanley Matthews, one of English football's greatest ambassadors. John Barnes *(below, right)* meets the maestro.

Steve McManaman was at his inspirational best at Wembley. The venue was the perfect stage for the youngster to display his skill. Here, Macca shrugs off Scott Green *(above)* before flashing home an unstoppable shot to open the scoring.

Coca-Cola

John Scales, one of the outstanding players of the season, prevails in this aerial duel with Bolton's Mixu Paatelainen.

Steve McManaman *(above)* was a handful all afternoon at Wembley as Richard Sneakes and Alan Thompson found out to their cost. Meanwhile, defender Phil Babb *(below)* takes a tumble as he holds off Bolton winger, David Lee.

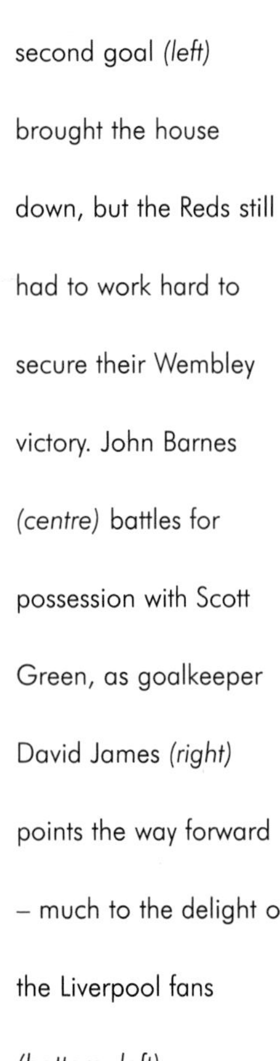

Steve McManaman's second goal *(left)* brought the house down, but the Reds still had to work hard to secure their Wembley victory. John Barnes *(centre)* battles for possession with Scott Green, as goalkeeper David James *(right)* points the way forward – much to the delight of the Liverpool fans *(bottom, left)*.

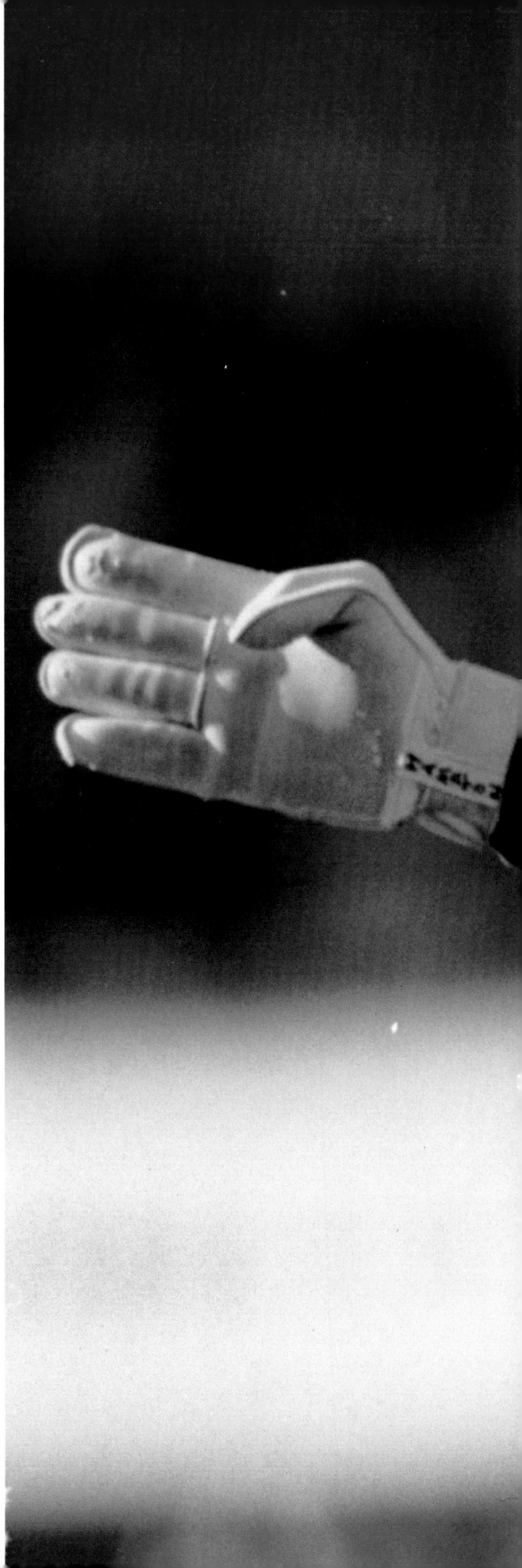

adidas
Carlsberg

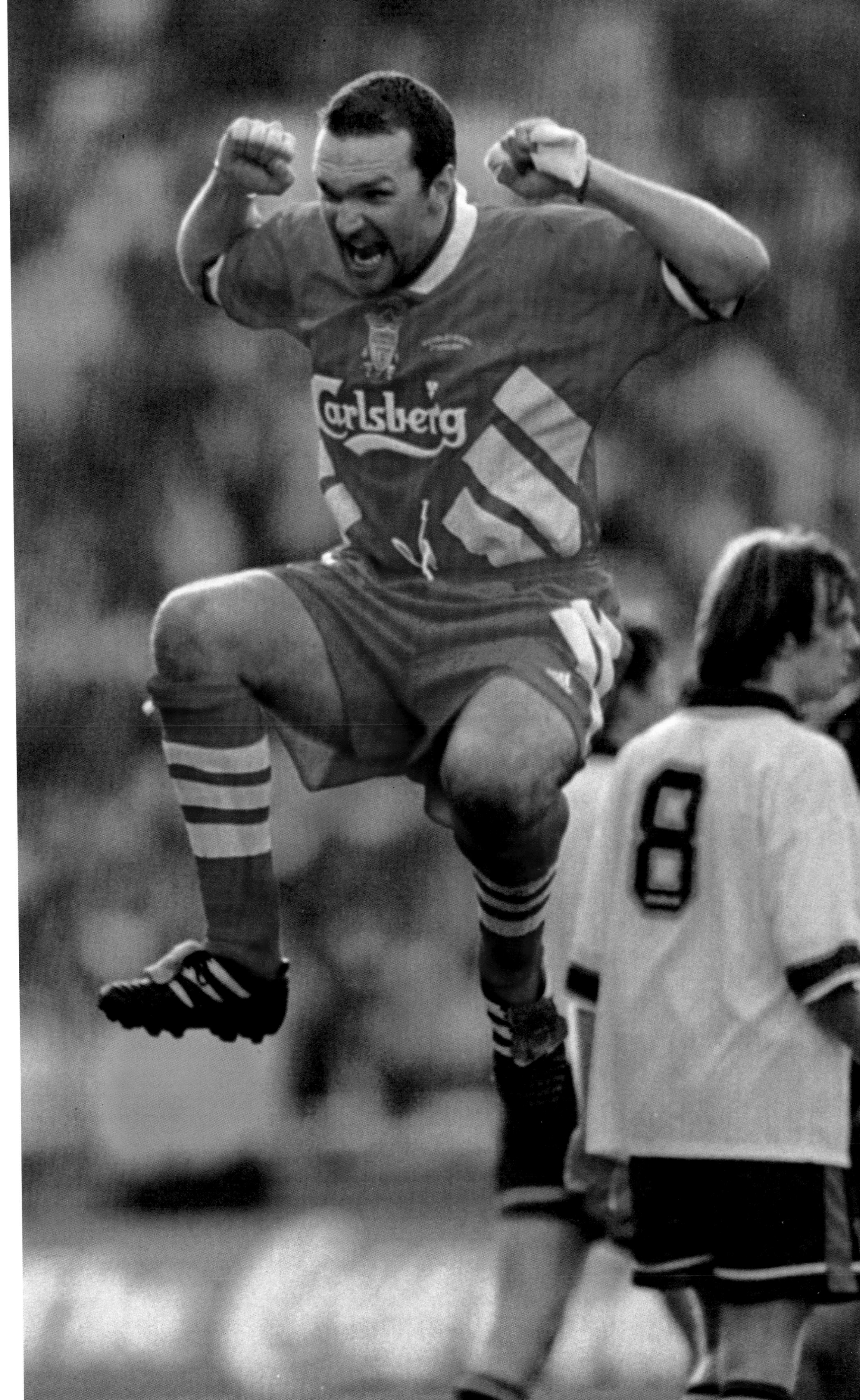


Robbie Fowler and Jamie Redknapp *(above, left)* parade the Coca-Cola Cup while Neil Ruddock *(right)* jumps for joy as the final whistle is blown. Even striking partners Ian Rush and Robbie Fowler *(below, left)* get in on the early celebrations.

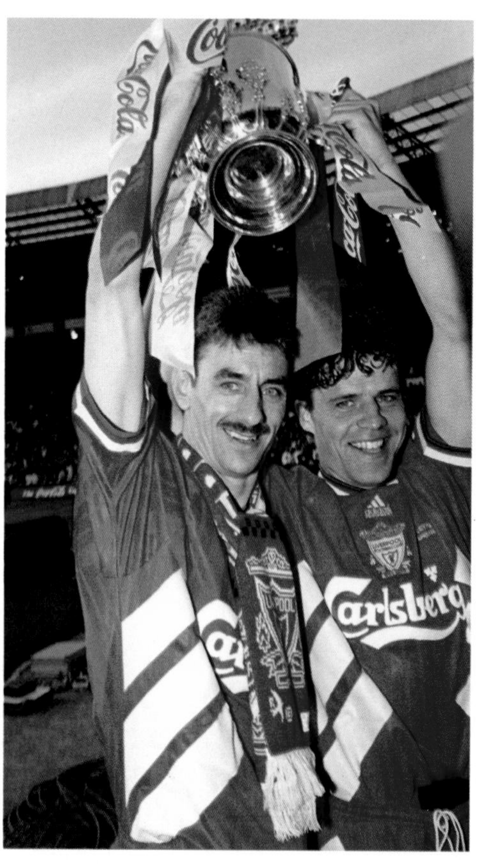

An elated Ian Rush asks Stig Inge Bjornebye to give him a helping hand in raising the Coca-Cola Cup *(above, far left)*. Two-goal Steve McManaman won the Man-of-the-Match award *(above, left and right)* and no one begrudged him this moment in the limelight – certainly not the fans *(left)*.

Coca-Cola

adidas
LIVERPOOL
FOOTBALL CLUB
EST. 1892

# 1994-1995

## GOING BACK TO THE BOOTROOM

LIVERPOOL'S first full season with Roy Evans in charge proved to be a revivalist campaign in every way, with the Coca-Cola Cup and a coveted place in Europe the fitting rewards for months of hard work.

It is said that success is often written in the stars. Perhaps it's not surprising then that one of the most respected figures in European football predicted a return to the glory days for the Reds, three weeks before the start of the 1994/95 campaign.

Giovanni Trapattoni was the elegant Italian who, as coach of Juventus, found himself in opposition to Liverpool in the ill-fated European Cup Final of 1984 at the Heysel Stadium. Like Liverpool, Trapattoni had come a long way since that painful night in Brussels.

He was now coach of German giants, Bayern Munich, and faced the Reds in starkly different circumstances. For this time it was a prestige friendly in Fulda, Germany. The date was 1 August 1994, and Liverpool were beginning their most rigorous pre-season tour for years.

Trapattoni admitted he was surprised that the Merseysiders were no longer dominating English football. After watching his side prevail 2-0 and taking into account Liverpool's lack of fitness at that stage, he said: *"They are clearly still a very good team. They may not be at their best at the moment, but the club has so much history and tradition, I believe they will be back."*

With seven Italian titles and a host of European and domestic cups under his belt, Trapattoni does not hand out plaudits lightly. His words would prove to be prophetic. For this would be the season that marked the rebirth of the Reds under Roy Evans.

It was reported that Danish defender, Torben Piechnik, was hoping to clinch a return to his home land with Aarhus or AGF Kontraktfodbold. Within weeks of the press reports hitting the streets, the defender would soon be heading out of Anfield.

John Barnes was looking fitter and leaner than ever after a summer of slimming. He shed nearly a stone after spending the close-season running and abstaining from junk food. Once more, he was looking like a mean dribbling machine. The England star was bold enough to predict a top three place for the Reds, providing they played the *"Liverpool way."*

The fans knew exactly what Barnes meant. For outsiders, he explained: *"If we can get our old passing game going again, I think we will finish in the top three. Definitely! We will have as good a squad as anyone, even if we don't bring new players in."* Such optimism captured the mood in the Liverpool camp as the pre-season action continued.

A 2-0 win over Borussia Moenchengladbach had preceded the Bayern defeat. Now the Reds faced a stern international test – against the Norwegian national side. Boss Evans handed a debut to Danish Under-21 'keeper, Michael Stensgaard, in an Oslo clash that was a farewell occasion for Norwegian World Cup skipper, Rune Bratseth.

The vastly experienced home side brushed aside an Ian Rush opener to win the game 3-1 with goals from Jahn Ivor Jakabsen, Oeyvind Leonhardsen and substitute Geir Frigard. Evans' main consolation was the performance of young Stensgaard in goal who displayed alertness and bravery.

But the manager was disappointed by the result. *"The one thing to our credit was that we did not throw in the towel,"* he said. *"But overall, it was one of our poorest performances."*

English teams normally select low key opposition pre-season. However, the Merseysiders were still edging towards full fitness and were being pushed to the limit by an array of quality sides. For Evans the time had come when he knew he must strengthen his squad at the earliest opportunity.

Soon 5 August had arrived and big defender, Neil Ruddock, had put the Oslo disappointment behind him to restate his international ambitions with England. At the same time, he backed the qualities of new coach Doug Livermore. *"I have a burning desire to play for England,"* said Ruddock. *"I believe Doug can help me. This is the third time I have worked under him. I was with him in the reserves at Spurs and then with the first team when I came back from Southampton.*

*"Doug has been one of the biggest influences on my career."*

Another testing friendly now loomed against SV Hamburg, the German outfit famous for signing Kevin Keegan from Liverpool in the late Seventies. Steve Harkness was named in a flat back four, but Evans did not rule out the possibility of trying a sweeper system in the coming season. The fans did not realise at the time just how significant this move would be.

The Anfield boss took time out to reject West Ham's offer of former left-back David Burrows for Don Hutchison. Elsewhere, former Liverpool 'keeper, Bruce Grobbelaar – now a free agent – was lining up a move to Southampton.

On the playing front, there was more disappointment as the Reds lost again. Hamburg triumphed 3-1 and the only crumbs of comfort were a Robbie Fowler penalty, a spirited second half revival and a determined Harkness performance as he battled to stake a claim for a first team place.

Liverpool lacked experienced cover at the back, having left Julian Dicks and Mark Wright at home. Dicks was overweight and Wright was told he had an attitude problem. Evans was demonstrating clearly that he was the boss. But he was forced to admit on tour that he was worried about the defence.

Things improved in the final foreign friendly on 8 August. Robbie Fowler scored a hat-trick in an emphatic victory over Hertha Berlin although Harkness was sent-off for a second bookable offence. It was only Liverpool's second victory in six warm-up games.

adidas
Carlsberg
adidas

adidas
Carlsberg
Carlsberg

Jamie Redknapp *(above, left)* seems to have lost his race with training partner Steve McManaman by a short neck. Elsewhere, it's all in a days training for the Liverpool squad.

Carlsberg

# AUGUST '94

## A TIME TO EXPERIMENT

ROY EVANS kicked off the season by experimenting with his defence. The boss opted for three centre-backs to hold things together, which enabled the fullbacks to push into midfield whenever possible. The one drawback was the lack of the right personnel at this stage. But skipper, Ian Rush, remained buoyant. *"The pre-season tour was difficult,"* he said. *"The heat and all the travelling did not help. You are always tired the day after a game and it takes 10 or 15 minutes to get going again on the pitch after a long journey. It's a case of needing to be a bit sharper mentally. But that will come with more matches."*

A boost came when Jan Molby declared himself match fit after an absence of some eight months. A domestic friendly at Wrexham was won 3-1. There was more good news when striker Nigel Clough also put his injury worries behind him.

Boss Evans now moved to strengthen the defence with a record bid for Coventry City's Republic of Ireland star Phil Babb who was valued at £3.5m. Liverpool were also being linked with another talented central defender in Wimbledon's John Scales.

The big 19 August kick-off loomed. Liverpool faced a trip to Crystal Palace. There would be no place in the squad for Clough or Mark Walters, but Molby was back after his long lay-off. Palace were given a footballing lesson, with the big Dane the architect behind a stunning 6-1 away victory.

Molby showed the way with an accurate 12th minute penalty. Steve McManaman skipped clear to make it 2-0. Fowler cashed in on Pitcher's mistake to make it three and while Armstrong grabbed a consolation goal, a Rush header and further efforts from McManaman and Redknapp left the Londoners gasping.

Afterwards Molby declared: *"The players are a lot wiser than they were at this stage last year, whether they are youngsters or the older ones. Everyone realises that it's all about standards which have been set for over 25 years. It's not just about winning the first three games. We all have to make sure we have a better go than last season."*

Liverpool had actually begun the previous year in blistering fashion, but finished eighth as well as suffering premature exits in Coca-Cola and FA Cup competitions. Staying power would be the key this time round.

The Coca-Cola Cup draw was now made and Liverpool were paired with First Division Burnley. But the next action was a league clash against London rivals Arsenal on 28 August. The Reds would win 3-0, with Robbie Fowler completing the Premiership's fastest-ever hat-trick.

In a hectic first half spell at Anfield, lasting all of four minutes 33 seconds, Fowler rocked England's David Seaman with a superb display of finishing. After 26 minutes, the youngster pounced on the rebound after Jamie Redknapp's free-kick came off team-mate Rush. Three minutes later, Fowler took a McManaman pass to drill left-footed past Seaman. And with just 30 minutes on the clock, the Liverpudlian secured the match ball when he scored from a narrow angle after the keeper had blocked his first attempt.

Fowler said: *"Everyone has been saying the second season is harder than the first, so I went out to prove to people I could still do it. I've scored four in two games, but it's not about me. The whole team played well."*

As August drew to a close, the good news factor began to take over at Anfield. John Barnes won a sensational England recall after masterminding Liverpool's superb start to the season. He was named in an 18-man squad for a Wembley friendly against the United States.

Down in Coventry, the frustrated Phil Babb now took matters into his own hands to secure the move he wanted. He finally made his transfer request official, saying: *"I felt an end had to be made to the on-going speculation as it was having an unsettling effect on both me and – as Club Captain – the rest of the team. I have considered everybody's view on this and I believe it is in the best interests of all parties that the speculation be put to the test. I have therefore tendered a transfer request."*

Liverpool were immediately given permission to speak to the player as they prepared for their third Premiership game of the season, a trip to Southampton.

The fans and the players put the Babb affair temporarily out of their thoughts to concentrate on the clash at the Dell. Former star 'keeper, Bruce Grobbelaar, was in opposition. It was a strange challenge for the man who spent 13 years at Anfield, winning 13 major honours along the way.

Robbie Fowler's fifth strike in three games, plus a solo effort from John Barnes, gave Liverpool only their seventh League success in 24 trips to the Dell. The Reds were a classy act in the first 45 minutes and clinical in the second period of play.

There was a certain amount of controversy about Fowler's opener. Referee Martin Bodenham refused to blow for a dubious handball against the impressive Barnes and then ignored Southampton's offside claims as McManaman's pass freed Fowler. The striker raced on to fire home through Grobbelaar's legs.

Barnes' effort was a real wonder goal, scored after 77 minutes. He found himself on the left of the penalty box, dribbled across four defenders and then dragged the ball back before placing a right foot shot past Grobbelaar. For once, the veteran 'keeper was lost for words. He had seen it many times before, of course, but the flamboyant star was not used to being on the receiving end.

The fans who travelled to the Dell roared their delight. The new Liverpool team was beginning to take shape. It would be a season of rich promise.

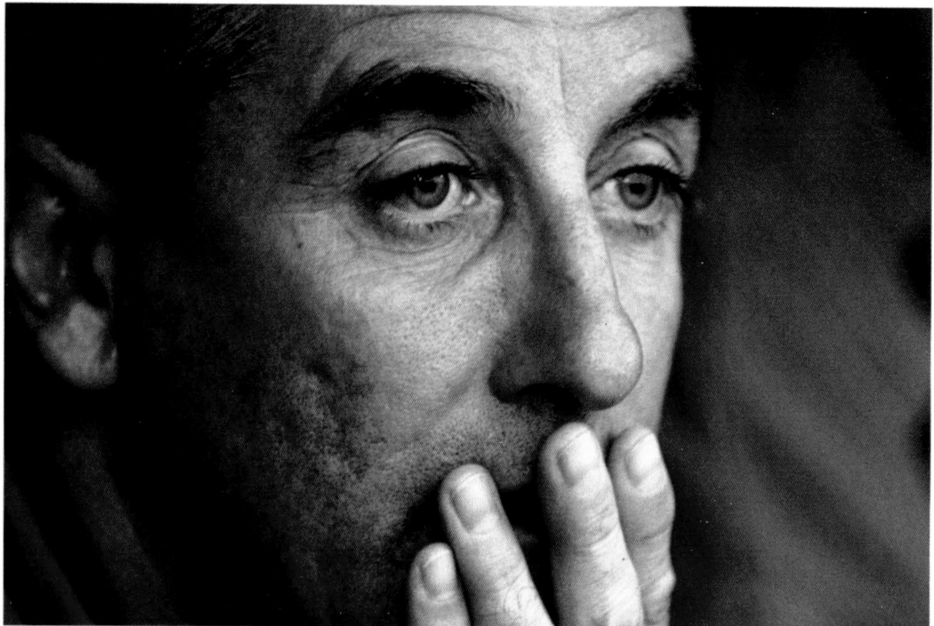

Roy Evans looks pensive on day one of the Premiership campaign. But the players soon had him beaming with their stunning victory at Palace. Stig Inge Bjornebye, meanwhile, gets into his stride against Arsenal while Robbie Fowler celebrates with Reds fans after his memorable treble against the Gunners.

Jamie Redknapp battled hard throughout the season to win over the Anfield faithful. In the end his skill, determination – and his infectious enthusiasm – won over the Kop. Here, Jamie warms up for the 28 August clash against Arsenal.

Jan Molby had a difficult season because of injury. But when the Danish international donned Liverpool's colours, his class always shone through. Robbie Fowler and Steve McManaman also had much to celebrate, as did Jamie Redknapp, who is caught battling it out with Chris Coleman of Crystal Palace *(above, right)*. And Steve Nicol finally brought down the curtain on a famous Anfield career. He displayed his true grit in the Premiership victory over Palace.

Carlsberg

JVC

Carlsberg

Carlsberg

Carlsberg

# SEPTEMBER '94

## BRITAIN'S COSTLIEST DEFENDER AT A COOL £3.6m

LIVERPOOL had secured three straight Premiership victories, scoring 11 goals and conceding just one. A measure of the club's ambition was that Roy Evans still felt it necessary to pay a British record transfer fee of £3.6m for a defender.

The boss heaped praise on his back four after the victory at Southampton and then revealed exactly why he had strengthened his hand still further. He said: *"Over a 42 game season, plus whatever there are in the cups, we certainly need another defender. But any defender should be pleased to keep clean sheets. Yesterday, at the Dell, our defenders did us proud. I was very pleased with their attitude."*

So why the swoop for Babb? *"He has proved his pace in the modern game,"* explained Evans. *"He's quite good in the air. In fact, he is good all round!"*

The manager's elation at concluding the deal was matched by that of the new arrival. Babb said: *"I think the club will establish itself again as the best Britain. There is no reason why Liverpool won't be the great side they were only a few years ago.*

*"The lads are on a high after their good start and we are all looking to get a major honour this season. People like Robbie Fowler, Jamie Redknapp, Rob Jones and myself are still learning the game. Where better to get your football education that at Anfield?"*

As if to doubly declare his ambition to put the Reds back in the trophy frame, boss Evans went out the following day and captured Wimbledon's talented centre-back, John Scales.

On 7 September, the revitalised John Barnes played for England against the United States at Wembley. The Liverpool star performed well in the 2-0 victory.

Back at Anfield, the big question was who – if anyone – would make way for new defenders Babb and Scales for the 10 September home game against West Ham? Evans agreed that *"no one deserved to be left out"*. At the same time, a manager is paid to make tough decisions...

Scales was the one who was given the first opportunity to shine with Babb restricted to the bench. The game finished goalless, although there was a flash point when former Everton striker, Tony Cottee, was dismissed after scything down Rob Jones.

Evans planned to use the following week to see how Babb shaped up in training. The manager declared that no one was under pressure. *"He will do what I want,"* said the boss. *"It gives me problems, but nice problems. Phil has got to come into the equation at some stage. We've got a week to work with him."*

As one of the biggest games of the season loomed an Old Trafford clash against Manchester United – Liverpool dismissed reports linking Jan Molby with Tranmere Rovers. Evans said: *"Jan is in our first team. Only two games ago, we were saying the Messiah had returned. He's still an important player to have around."*

There was also speculation about the future of one of the club's great servants, Steve Nicol. The 32-year-old Scot had been unfortunate to lose his place to Scales. Evans recognised that fact when he said: *"At some stage, we will have to decide what is good for Liverpool and for Steve Nicol. He should have that option for the great service he has given us."*

Meanwhile, there was still no announcement concerning Babb's possible full debut.

The weekend showdown with United cost the Reds their unbeaten record. Goals from Andrei Kanchelskis and Brian McClair gave United a flattering 2-0 victory. The Reds had named an unchanged side with Babb still on the bench. Ironically, the game turned in United's favour after Babb replaced Molby in midfield after 71 minutes, at which stage the match was goalless. Evans accepted that the substitution possibly worked against Liverpool on the day. But it is always easy to be wise after the event.

On Wednesday 21 September, Liverpool prepared themselves for the Coca-Cola Cup second round, first leg tie against Burnley at Anfield. Evans once again named an unchanged side with no place in his line-up for Babb.

He felt it necessary to explain the situation once again, saying: *"Phil is a good pro. He knows it's all about Liverpool and that he will get his chance. I don't expect him to be totally pleased with the situation. He is out of the team at the moment, but when he is in, he will become a regular."*

The Burnley game was fairly tough against lively First Division opposition, but a precise header from John Scales from a Jamie Redknapp cross and a close range strike from Robbie Fowler gave the Merseysiders a solid first leg advantage.

Skipper Ian Rush now paid a special tribute to Liverpool's "secret weapon." In a special salute to giant goalkeeper, David James, the Welsh striker said: *"He has been absolutely brilliant. David was in and out of the team last year because he was inconsistent, even though we all knew he was a good 'keeper.*

*"I think he felt that, even if he had a good game, Bruce Grobbelaar would win his place back. Now Bruce has gone and David has taken his chance with both big hands. He has been dominant at corners and has literally looked head and shoulders above everyone when jumping for the ball. I can tell you that strikers think twice about challenging him when they see someone of his size up against them."*

Liverpool now faced another stern test of character with a trip to Newcastle. The big news was that Babb was finally on course for his full debut. The match against the rising Geordies finished 1-1. In many ways, it was a moral victory for the Reds because Newcastle were being tipped by many as title favourites and had secured six successive Premiership wins under former Anfield favourite, Kevin Keegan. Robert Lee scored for the home side with Ian Rush equalising for the Reds after 70 minutes.

adidas
Carlsberg
adidas
Carlsberg

adidas
Carlsberg
adidas
Carlsberg
Lucozade

Games against Manchester United are traditionally fierce and competitive. And John Barnes and Paul Ince *(above)* certainly didn't need any encouragement in the no-holds-barred Premiership clash at Old Trafford. It was a hectic afternoon all round in front of a typically partisan United crowd.

Liverpool's Rob Jones comes out on top in his battle with United's Lee Sharpe. The England defender keeps his head and clears the ball away from the Reds goal despite intense United pressure.

For style and sheer determination, Steve McManaman takes some beating. Here, caught in action against Newcastle United, Macca comes close to scoring against Magpies at St. James' Park. The game finished all square, at one goal a piece.

Ian Rush was the Liverpool scorer at Newcastle. Here *(left)*, he shows a clean pair of heels to his marker. And, in the clash against the other United *(below, left)* Robbie Fowler goes shoulder to shoulder against Manchester's Steve Bruce, while David James *(below, right)* does his best to look as though he's on the ball.

# OCTOBER '94

## IS IT A BIRD? IS IT A PLANE? NO, IT'S SUPERMAC!

STEVE McMANAMAN had not scored at home for two years. Perhaps the Owls of Sheffield should have been wise enough to realise that someone, somewhere, was going to suffer for Supermac's goal drought. Wednesday found themselves on the wrong end of a 4-1 hiding as the Reds opened October in style.

Former Tranmere Rovers defender, Ian Nolan, returned to Merseyside in a Wednesday shirt and shocked the Anfield crowd by snatching a 33rd minute opener. But it was downhill all the way for the visitors after that. Liverpool equalised after 51 minutes with a little help from opposing 'keeper, Kevin Pressman, who failed to hold a 20 yard shot from Stig Inge Bjornebye. It presented Ian Rush with the simplest of close range opportunities.

Rush's equaliser contrasted with McManaman's stunning effort that gave the Reds the lead. The youngster went on a mazy run past three defenders before rifling home a right foot shot. There was an element of fortune about McManaman's second, which deflected off Des Walker and looped over the helpless Pressman after 66 minutes. Steve ensured he would be taking the match ball home when he slotted home Phil Babb's low cross two minutes before the end.

Incredibly, the young player's tremendous form failed to win him an immediate England call for the friendly against Romania. Team-mate Babb said: *"I wouldn't like to be playing against Steve right now. With his style of wing play, he is on a par with Ryan Giggs. We are going to call him 'Snake Hips McManaman'. He should definitely have been called up by England."*

On Wednesday 5 October, Liverpool played their Coca-Cola Cup second round return at Burnley, seeking to protect a 2-0 first leg advantage. Nigel Clough was given his first start of the season as the Merseysiders hammered home the gulf in class between the sides with a 4-1 triumph.

Jamie Redknapp showed tremendous footwork to beat the keeper and slot home the first. Robbie Fowler cashed in on a Stig Inge Bjornebye cross after 50 minutes, his eighth goal in seven Coca-Cola ties. Redknapp caught the 'keeper napping at the near post after 67 minutes, and Clough produced an excellent volley to leave Burnley reeling. A late Robinson goal was scant consolation for the home side.

England boss, Terry Venables, now chose to watch Liverpool at Anfield against Aston Villa. The 3-2 home victory owed much to the ever-improving Robbie Fowler who found the net twice. He was ably supported by Neil Ruddock. The Reds now revealed that they had offered McManaman a new a four year deal. The player celebrated by finally claiming a place in the England squad for the Romania game. Ruddock, John Barnes and Rob Jones were also in the international party.

Acting England Under-21 manager, Kevin Keegan, suggested that Robbie Fowler would soon be joining his team-mates in the senior squad. Keegan was speaking up for the young striker after he was sent-off during the 3-1 win over Austria in a European Under-21 Championships qualifying game. ""*Robbie didn't do anything wrong,"* said Keegan. *"It happened because the ref changed his mind. At the start, he was ruling things as fouls and then started to let them go. Robbie just got frustrated.*

*"I thought he worked very hard throughout the game. In fact, he never stopped working. He had a hand in two goals and I was very impressed. I think he can easily bridge the gap to the next stage."*

Jamie Redknapp was the real Under-21 hero. The Reds' midfielder scored all three goals and Keegan said: *"Jamie gave a real captain's example. He took his goals with confidence and if the free-kick at the end had been scored by a Brazilian, we would have all been raving about it."*

Liverpool now travelled to Ewood Park to test themselves against Blackburn. A Fowler goal and a John Barnes strike could not prevent two-goal Chris Sutton helping Rovers to come from behind to win 3-2. How vital those points would eventually be for Rovers in the final Championship reckoning.

Barnes shrugged of the defeat saying: *"I think we can still improve. We have a lot of young players. Jones, McManaman and Fowler can only get better. I think that with the quality of youngsters at Anfield, there's only one way Liverpool can go and that's up."*

Boss Evans spoke of the importance of rebuilding Anfield into an impenetrable fortress. He said: *"We want to make clubs fearful of Anfield because of our team and the support of our crowd. It's important to pick up home points. Everybody likes to think that their ground is a place where other sides find it hard to play."*

As if to emphasise the point, the Reds now crushed a depleted Wimbledon 3-0 in front of the Kop with goals from McManaman, Fowler and Barnes. The news after the game concerned the appointment of former Manchester City and England star, Joe Corrigan, to the position of goalkeeping coach. A delighted Corrigan said: *"It tremendous to be working for such a great club."*

Liverpool's Coca-Cola Cup chase gained momentum with a 2-1 third round home win over Stoke. Skipper Ian Rush was the two goal hero. The result earned the Reds a tough fourth round test at Blackburn. Manager Evans described it as: *"A great tie."* He added: *"We are going to have to play the top teams at some stage."*

McManaman gave the club a boost by signing the three-and-a-half-year deal he had been offered. Evans said: *"It's nice to get our young players signed up and it augers well for the future."*

The month ended with a fine 3-1 win at struggling Ipswich, followed by a 2-1 reversal in London against QPR. There was clearly some work still to be done, but the Reds were very much on the right lines with their young stars beginning to shine.

McEWAN'S
LAGER

John Barnes *(top, left)* is too skilful for Sheffield Wednesday's Graham Hyde. October was a hectic month, but scoring is always a moment to savour. And even the referee appears to be satisfied after Robbie Fowler's goal against Aston Villa *(above, right)*.

Goals don't come any better than John Barnes' spectacular bicycle kick against Blackburn on 15 October *(right)*. Ian Rush *(below)* tried to match him with a neat chip at QPR at the end of the month, but the ball failed to find the mark. Barnes was eventually the man on target again in the Loftus Road showdown.

Sheffield Wednesday 'keeper Kevin Pressman and Reds striker Ian Rush battle it out at Anfield *(above)*, while Neil Ruddock makes a determined challenge to thwart a Blackburn attack *(right)*.

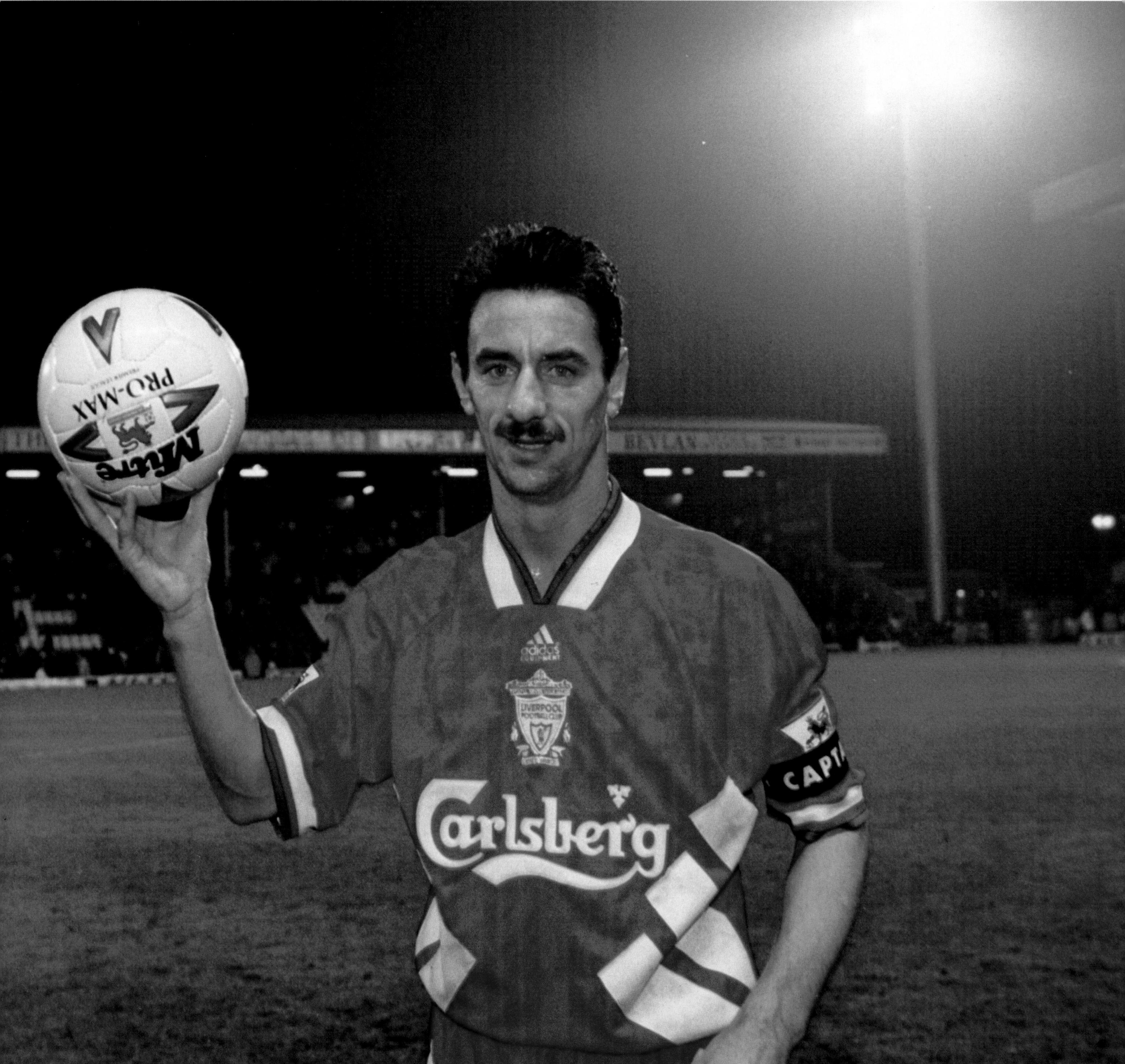
PRO-MAX
Mitre
adidas
LIVERPOOL FOOTBALL CLUB
Carlsberg

# NOVEMBER '94

## REMEMBER, REMEMBER, THE FIFTH OF NOVEMBER

A BONFIRE night clash against Nottingham Forest, who came to Anfield with an unbeaten Premiership away record, signalled the arrival of the month of November. Hard-working Liverpool returned to winning ways with a 1-0 victory. Robbie Fowler flicked home after Jamie Redknapp had flashed in a shot. The 14th minute goal proved decisive. Forest clearly missed the power of star striker, Stan Collymore, who watched from the sidelines with a hamstring problem. Little did Collymore realise that he would be signing for Liverpool on his next visit to Anfield. But this was all for the future.

For now, the fans were reflecting on Phil Babb's best performance in a Red jersey. Steve McManaman picked up on it when he said: *"I thought Phil played particularly well. He made a couple of great interceptions and I think his confidence must be sky high."*

Babb kept his feet on the ground, saying: *"I'm still a long way off my best. I've got a lot to offer. I'm still young and you're not supposed to reach your peak until your 27. I feel I'm restricted in that wide position. The bench don't like me galloping forward as much as I would like to. I think they want me to play well and get some games under my belt first. But Saturday was a step in the right direction."*

While rivals Everton were exchanging managers, Liverpool were getting on with the job in hand under the highly efficient Evans. The Reds beat Chelsea 3-1 on 9 November, and while it was not a top drawer display, it was emphatic enough. The visitors had Erland Johnsen sent off after 72 minutes after he raised an arm to Neil Ruddock.

But the worst thing Chelsea did was open the scoring through John Spencer after three minutes. The Reds powered back and Robbie Fowler pounced onto a superb Jan Molby though ball to equalise. Fowler headed a second from Rob Jones' cross, with Ruddock claiming the third after 24 minutes with a fine downward header.

John Barnes now revealed that he wanted to finish his career at Anfield. He said: *"I'm hoping the club will offer me a new contract. I would definitely like to stay for another three or four years...longer, if possible."*

Barnes, Ruddock and Jones were named in the England side to met Nigeria on Wednesday 15 November. England won 1-0 and the Anfield bonus was that Steve McManaman came on after 21 minutes for Robert Lee.

Robbie Fowler also enjoyed a very special night when he collected his Liverpool Echo Merseyside Sports Personality of the Year award at a city centre ceremony.

The big local derby now focused the thoughts of players and fans alike. Liverpool, vibrant and lively all season, found themselves caught up in a typical battle at Goodison Park. Duncan Ferguson rose to head Everton's opener after 56 minutes. Paul Rideout slid home from eight yards to confirm a 2-0 home victory.

Roy Evans said: *"Everton didn't cause us too many problems at the back. We got into positions to equalise, but we spurned those chances."*

Jamie Redknapp, left out of the line-up for the derby clash against Everton, hammered home his determination to stay and fight for his place. He said: *"All I want to do is pull on that red shirt. I have got to bounce back from this disappointment."*

On 26 November, Neil Ruddock scored a second half own goal against his old club, Tottenham Hotspur, to cancel out Robbie Fowler's 39th minute spot-kick.

Meanwhile, the determined Redknapp had secured the place he coveted, replacing hamstring victim Jan Molby in the first team. Steve McManaman was sent tumbling by Campbell after 39 minutes and Fowler thumped the resulting penalty into the back of the Spurs net. The Reds played well and were on course for victory until Campbell broke powerfully down the left after 77 minutes. Ruddock mistimed his intervention and put the ball in the back of his own net. The game finished 1-1.

It was now announced that Paul Stewart's proposed move to Wolves was off. He returned from his loan spell after developing groin trouble. Graham Taylor, manager of the First Division outfit, said: *"Paul has been very unfortunate. But I can't go ahead and sign someone who is injured. He wouldn't pass the medical."*

As the month drew to a close, former manager Kenny Dalglish spoke about his old playing partner, Ian Rush, as Blackburn prepared to face Liverpool in the Coca-Cola Cup fourth round tie at Ewood Park. *"Ian is the best player I have ever played with,"* said Dalglish. *"He has not missed many games and he certainly never went missing in the ones we played in together.*

*"It's a tremendous number of appearances for a striker and some record. Ian has set a standard for anyone who is going to play for Liverpool. You would think the number of goals he has scored in the number of games he has played would be impossible to beat."*

The Rush record was truly impressive: 326 goals scored in 599 games for the Reds. Was Dalglish looking into a crystal ball when he paid tribute to his old pal? As it turned out, Rush grabbed a hat-trick in the Reds' stunning 3-1 Cup success against Rovers. The old master eclipsed Blackburn's young pretenders, the highly priced Alan Shearer and Chris Sutton.

Rush opened the scoring with a rasping shot after 19 minutes from a Fowler pass. He ran onto Rob Jones' pass after 57 minutes to fire the second and when Stig Inge Bjornebye's centre was poorly headed out by Graham Le Saux after 73 minutes, the great Anfield predator completed his treble. Sutton scored a late consolation goal for Rovers but the morning newspaper headlines were about the unstoppable Rush. Kenny Dalglish simply stood in the wings and shook his head knowingly. He had seen it all before. There is simply no substitute for real class.

John Barnes and his young son receive an award from Liverpudlian comedy star Jimmy Tarbuck *(above, right)*.

Meanwhile, Jamie Redknapp *(above, left)* Rob Jones *(bottom, left)* and John Barnes *(right)* are the action men

in the Bonfire Night clash with Forest.

Carlsberg
Coors

HOLSTEN
Carlsberg

Spurs proved to be tough opponents. And Mark Walters and Dean Austin *(far left)* make sure there's no quarter given or taken as they sprint after the ball. Macca *(above)* takes a refreshing break. But it's all go for Rob Jones *(left)* and Jamie Redknapp *(below)*.

Carlsberg

Carlsberg

Blackburn were outgunned in the Coca-Cola Cup at Ewood Park. Ian Rush blasts home *(above, left)* and celebrates in style as a memorable hat-trick unfolds *(below, left)*. The Welsh star had tremendous support from partner Robbie Fowler *(above)* who shows courage by beating England rival Alan Shearer to a header. The Reds won win the tie emphatically to continue their march on Wembley.

Sytnor of

# DECEMBER '94

## GUNNING FOR WEMBLEY WITH A TOUGH QUARTER FINAL DRAW

LIVERPOOL and Arsenal were pitted against each other at Anfield when the Coca-Cola Cup reached the quarter-final stages. Manager Roy Evans recognised the threat posed by the Londoners. He said: *"Arsenal have probably been the top cup team over the past four or five years. Blackburn was difficult, but this will be just as tough."*

But the bookmakers chose to ignore the caution shown by the Reds boss and immediately installed the Merseysiders as 5-2 favourites to lift the Cup.

Liverpool were now rocked by a double injury blow, with the Jones' boys on the receiving end. England full-back, Rob, was ruled out of the Premiership clash at Coventry with a hamstring problem while it was revealed that young striker, Lee, had broken his leg playing for the reserves.

December's action began with a 1-1 draw at Coventry. The Reds squandered an early lead to allow Sean Flynn to score an equaliser and cap a spirited second half Coventry revival. Rush's second minute goal had given the visitors a dream start. But subsequent events were to frustrate the Liverpool players.

Neil Ruddock described the performance as the side's worst to date. He said: *"Once we scored, we should have killed them off. We felt tired after Wednesday, but you have to cope with that. The manager wasn't happy. He was entitled to have a go – and he did."*

Ian Rush was preparing for his big Testimonial game against Celtic. Over 8,000 Scots were heading to Merseyside.

Dalglish had agreed to play in the game and recreate the famous partnership. It was a night for Rush to savour. Liverpool won 6-0, with substitute Dalglish as magical as ever. Rush blossomed in the presence of his former partner to score a goal that brought the house down.

He said: *"It was a very emotional night and I never dreamed I would receive such a reception. It was absolutely fantastic, made even better when both sets of fans sang my name."*

Around the country, people were beginning to take note of Roy Evans' Anfield revival. England coach, Terry Venables, led the praise after naming six Liverpool players in his 'B' squad for a game against the Republic of Ireland. He said: "There is no doubt Liverpool are going through a period when things are looking very good for them. That's due to the players who have been in the side and who are developing. They've got a lot of new faces, a lot of younger players and it's working well.

*"I hope I can enjoy the same sort of success through these players. Judging by the amount of times the word Liverpool appears on the squad lists, it seems to be the case that Liverpool are bringing on English players."*

Steve McManaman and Neil Ruddock, who had won full caps against Nigeria, were named in the 'B' squad along with David James, John Scales, Robbie Fowler and Jamie Redknapp.

But despite the praise and international recognition, Liverpool had injury problems as they prepared to face Crystal Palace at Anfield. McManaman, Jones, Molby and Rush were all on the treatment table. The injury list took its toll against a well-drilled Palace side that had improved dramatically since that opening day 6-1 defeat against the Reds. This time, a goalless draw was the end product.

Ruddock captained the England 'B' side against the Republic and was able to reflect on his second international clean sheet. He was the star performer in a solid 2-0 display in which Andy Cole, of Manchester United, and home-based Robbie Fowler were the scorers.

Ruddock said: *"Keeping the clean sheet was important and captaining the side was a great honour. I love the responsibility. I feel I did well and I've just got to keep it going."*

As the month unfolded, Liverpool travelled to Chelsea for a pre-Christmas confrontation. The goalless draw was no classic, but there was no lack of effort from the players.

On 23 December, Mark Wright appeared ready to begin his latest comeback campaign after six months in the shadows. He had undergone a spell of rehabilitation at the Lilleshall Training Centre and boss Evans said: *"Mark has been to see a specialist and will hopefully be able to resume light training again. It has been a frustrating time for him."*

Liverpool would recover from two goalless draws to win 2-1 at Leicester on Boxing Day. The reappearance of Steve McManaman was a timely Christmas present and he constantly had the home defence in disarray. 'Keeper David James was the hero of the day, diving to his left to save Steve Thompson's spot kick after 64 minutes.

It was the turning point because Liverpool were awarded a penalty of their own three minutes later, giving Fowler the chance to ram home his 16th Premiership goal of the season. Fowler turned creator after 78 minutes to enable Ian Rush to increase the lead. Leicester grabbed a late consolation goal through Roberts, but the visitors had three crucial points in the bag.

On 28 December, Liverpool beat Manchester City 2-0 at Anfield with Steve McManaman in great form. Fowler and Phelan (og) were the men on target.

Port Vale failed with an audacious bid to land Steve Nicol and Mark Wright on loan. Liverpool concentrated on the action with a tremendous New Year's Eve win at Leeds A rocket free-kick from Jamie Redknapp gave the Reds the lead and Fowler added a second – his 20th goal of the season. The hat-trick of Christmas victories over Leicester, Manchester City and Leeds delighted everyone at the club. It was already shaping up to being a Happy New Year.

It's the Ian Rush slide show as he pounces to score against Celtic during his Testimonial game at Anfield *(right)*. The emphatic final scoreline highlighted Liverpool's determination to put one over on their famous Scottish rivals. Rush's delight at his own contribution is all too clear *(below)*.

Kenny Dalglish *(left)* turned back the clock when he returned to Anfield to salute his old playing partner, Ian Rush. The former Reds sorcerer was soon weaving his magic spell and enjoying every minute of Rushie's Testimonial. For his part, Ian proved that goalscoring is kid's stuff *(above)*.

Liverpool enjoyed a stroll at Elland Road on New Year's Eve, winning the Premiership clash against Leeds by two goals to nil. It was a team effort all the way. Robbie Fowler *(above, left)* scored in the victory and even the experienced Gordon Strachan *(below, left)* couldn't spark a revival from the Yorkshiremen. Skill in midfield and strength in defence also inspired wins over Leicester and Manchester City.

Jamie Redknapp was on song against Leeds. When the England Under 21 star's superb free-kick hit the back of the net, the visiting fans' New Year celebrations got off to a flying start.

adidas
Carlsberg
UMBRO

# JANUARY '95

## OVER THE MOON ABOUT SHINING STARS

MANAGER Roy Evans was delighted with the Reds' Christmas return of a maximum nine points. But he knew three more tough matches were looming – including a crucial FA Cup third round test and a Coca-Cola Cup quarter final. This encouraged him to keep his feet firmly on the ground.

*"We are not in the title driving seat,"* declared Evans. *"Manchester United and Blackburn are. But we have done ourselves no harm at all in the last three matches. If the others slip, we can take advantage. It's just a case of keeping the pressure on.*

*Evans looked to his experienced stars to continue setting the standards, saying: "John Barnes and Ian Rush were shining examples to the youngsters in the victory at Elland Road. Barnes was outstanding again, but he has been like that all season. Robbie Fowler has been getting the goals, but Ian Rush's work rate against Leeds was unbelievable. If we keep performing like that, we have the chance to go on and become a real team."*

On Tuesday 3 January, a dark cloud was hanging over Anfield following the news that up-and-coming midfielder, Ian Frodsham, 18, had died following his long battle against cancer. Ian had been tipped to go all the way in the game, having represented England at junior level. He passed away, holding his mum's hand and surrounded by his devoted family, at his home in Kirkby.

His father, John, said: *"Ian was brave to the end. This past year has been a nightmare for us. But throughout it all, Ian never gave up."*

The whole of the club mourned the likeable youngster who had been Liverpool through and through. The best possible salute would be for the team to go out and win the next game, a home test against Norwich. The 4-0 scoreline – and the manner in which it was achieved – was a fitting tribute to Ian Frodsham.

News now broke that rivals Manchester United had paid £7m for Newcastle's Andy Cole. United had previously been tracking Nottingham Forest hitman, Stan Collymore, and Liverpool now registered their interest in the star. Out on the pitch, the Reds were held to a goalless FA Cup third round draw against spirited Birmingham City.

As the Reds prepared for their Coca-Cola Cup clash against Arsenal, Evans denied he was planning a summer swoop for QPR's Les Ferdinand. All would become clear in the months ahead.

Arsenal arrived on Merseyside with their manager making more headlines than the team. George Graham was being investigated by the Premier League regarding transfer irregularities. Both teams concentrated on the football. Liverpool won 1-0, but the scoreline did not do them justice. They outclassed their opponents, who went behind after 59 minutes when John Barnes touched a free-kick to Neil Ruddock. The defender threaded the ball to Ian Rush and the alert skipper slotted home an exquisitely created goal.

Bookmakers William Hill now made the Reds 4-6 odds on favourites to win the Cup after they had been drawn to meet Crystal Palace in the semi-finals. Bolton and Swindon would contest the other tie.

In the middle of the month, Liverpool suffered a surprise home set-back against relegation-threatened Ipswich Town. Adam Tanner's first half goal separated the teams as the Merseysiders suffered their first home defeat of the season.

It was also announced that Evans had been handed a two-year extension to his existing contract which still had 18 months to run. Chief Executive, Peter Robinson, commented: *"The board have been delighted with Roy's work since he took over."* A pleased Evans added: *"I'm delighted with the offer, but let's not get too carried away. There is still a lot of work to be done."*

Birmingham arrived at Anfield for a fascinating FA Cup replay. The Reds had to rely on a penalty shoot-out to gain safe passage to the fourth round. The scoring opened after 21 minutes when a Jamie Redknapp effort rebounded off Bennett to give the Reds the lead. Ricky Otto equalised for City to set-up a spot-kick showdown.

The Second Division side missed four penalties and Liverpool 'keeper, David James, became an instant hero. Jamie Redknapp and Stig Inge Bjornebye kept their cool from the spot and Liverpool moved through. James said: *"I guessed right in the shoot-out. Maybe I'll guess the National Lottery numbers this week!"*

On Saturday 21 June, veteran Steve Nicol finally ended his 13 year relationship with the club when he linked up with Howard Kendall at Notts County. Nicol said: *"It's a wrench to leave. I've had some marvellous times, but all good things must come to an end."*

On the same day, Liverpool's game at Wimbledon was postponed because of a waterlogged pitch. The break was a boost for Ian Rush who was scheduled to miss the clash due to bruised ribs. He could now concentrate on getting fit in time for the big Anfield clash against Everton.

The derby clash proved to be a game in which tackling triumphed over technique. After a goalless draw, John Barnes suggested: *"We need to change our style. When we play teams who come and get men behind the ball, we tend to stand in there with them instead of being patient, trying to pull them out of position. I think we have to reassess our play."*

It was one big game after another. On 28 January, the Reds featured in another goalless draw, this time at Burnley in the fourth round of the FA Cup. Boss Evans demanded more goals from his shot-shy team – not just from the strikers, but from all departments!

The month ended on a positive note with Steve McManaman named Merseyside Sports Personality of the Year by Liverpool Echo readers.

Whether it was in the air or on the ground, Liverpool had their eye on the ball during January. The case for the defence was offered by Stig Inge Bjornebye against Birmingham *(top, right)*, while Norwich City's Ian Crook found Steve McManaman too hot to handle *(above, right)*.

Liverpool figured in tough FA and Coca-Cola Cup ties during January and managed to maintain their double assault on domestic honours. Although Arsenal succumbed easily enough at Anfield, lesser lights Birmingham and Burnley didn't give up without a fight.

Carlsberg
adidas

It took a penalty shoot-out to settle the FA Cup drama against Birmingham City. Liverpool 'keeper David James *(above)* was up to the penalty challenge as was midfielder Jamie Redknapp (bottom). Brum were glum *(centre)*, but Steve McManaman was on Cloud Nine *(left)*.

# FEBRUARY '95

## FRIEND OR FOE? STAN PROVES A POINT

AT THE START of February, Roy Evans dismissed a report that he was planning to sign Dutch international defender, Ronald Koeman, from Barcelona. But it was an open secret that the Liverpool boss admired the qualities of Nottingham Forest's Stan Collymore. As the Reds prepared to meet Forest at the City Ground, Neil Ruddock assessed the opponent who, in a matter of months, was destined to become an £8.5m team-mate.

Ruddock said: *"From what I have seen, Collymore is a very good player. He's strong, pacy and he scores goals with both feet. He might think he has got nothing to prove against us. But if Liverpool are to maintain their interest in him, he must keep doing what he has been doing all season. The gaffer will be able to get a close look at Collymore, but hopefully he won't play well.*

*"He is certainly good enough to play for Liverpool. If he keeps going the way he has, he will definitely play for England. That would benefit the national team and also benefit us if he signed."*

On cue, Collymore gave Forest the lead after Barnes' pass was intercepted by Scott Gemmill. Ian Woan and Bryan Roy continued the move before Collymore netted from close range.

Things looked decidedly tricky for the Reds when Phil Babb was sent-off for tripping an opponent. But Robbie Fowler fired a deserved injury time equaliser, taking a Steve McManaman flicked pass and drilling home.

Burnley arrived on Merseyside for the FA Cup fourth round replay. There was a minute's silence before the game for Sir John Smith – Liverpool's Chairman during many glorious campaigns – and Ken Addison, the club's former Development Manager. The loss of these two great Anfield servants was felt by everyone at Anfield.

John Barnes' first half header was enough to beat the Clarets and set up a fifth round showdown with Wimbledon. Neil Ruddock was dismissed after 81 minutes in an incident that probably saved the game. He clipped Liam Robinson's heel as the forward raced clear. It was an instinctive reaction, but Burnley were far from happy.

A Premiership clash at home to Queens Park Rangers followed. The Reds made amends for a poor first half performance with a John Scales goal that wiped out Kevin Gallen's sixth minute opener.

Manager Evans found himself dismissing speculation that defender Ruddock might be joining Scottish giants, Glasgow Rangers. He said: *"There has been no contact from Rangers. In any case, there would be no point. He's not for sale."*

Could Liverpool now make a giant stride towards Wembley? They faced Crystal Palace at Anfield in a Coca-Cola Cup semi-final, first leg. Robbie Fowler was the hero with a late strike that stunned the visitors. Steve McManaman's cross rebounded off Ian Rush, and Fowler sent a crashing right foot shot into the back of the net.

Afterwards a delighted Scales said: *"You can't knock Robbie. He is a great little player who is always looking for goals. He proved that against Nottingham Forest recently. He never dropped his head. I think his goal will prove vital."*

Another equally important knockout challenge loomed, this time in the fifth round of the FA Cup against the Dons. The game was just one minute and 51 seconds old when Andy Clarke silenced Anfield by rolling a low, right foot shot wide of David James.

The Reds had to pick themselves up off the floor and their spirit was rewarded when Fowler thumped home Bjornebye's cross after 33 minutes to make it 1-1. However, the lively visitors were desperately unlucky when Earle hit the post a minute from time. Evans remained optimistic about the replay, saying: *"It's not over yet. We gave ourselves a bit to do after losing an early goal. That made things difficult, but again we showed character. We got on with it and worked really hard. People talk about pride for your jersey. That is what we have got. They lads don't want to lose. One of these days, someone will pay the price."*

Games were coming thick and fast. Thankfully there was a respite when the Coca-Cola Cup return at Crystal Palace was postponed because of a waterlogged pitch.

The next game was on 25 February, a tricky test at Sheffield Wednesday. Former England winger, Chris Waddle, spoke about the qualities of Steve McManaman who was just beginning his international career. *"He is very positive when he picks up the ball,"* said Waddle. *"He will get to the bye-line, but he's more of a passer than a crosser. He has quick feet. Steve has got one thing on his mind when he runs and that is to cause danger. That's what I like about him. Every defender hates it when someone takes them on and forces them to run backwards."*

Liverpool overcame a David James injury and a Chris Bart-Williams goal to record a 2-1 Hillsborough triumph. John Barnes' 41st minute equaliser was just reward for the Reds' approach in a low key match in which James battled on bravely with a knee injury. McManaman won the match with a curling left foot shot after 59 minutes.

The final game of the month was the keenly awaited FA Cup replay at Wimbledon. Golden oldies John Barnes and Ian Rush were the heroes in a 2-0 success. At the seventh attempt, Rush finally equalled Denis Law's record post-war FA Cup goal tally of 41. For the record, he darted onto Barnes' near post pass to turn home a killer strike.

Former Dons defender Scales added: *"John has adapted brilliantly to his central midfield role and Ian was outstanding. People seem to write off older pros if they have had a half bad season. But age is no barrier if players look after themselves."*

Robbie Fowler was on target during February's 1-1 draw with Nottingham Forest at the City Ground. The Reds remained unbeaten during a productive month in both League and Cup competitions.

Neil Ruddock makes a point to the referee at Forest, although the official had his own thoughts on Razor's interpretation of the laws. But the Reds simply could not relax as February was notable for the tense Cup affairs against Burnley, Crystal Palace and Wimbledon.

Carlsberg

Neil Ruddock shows little regard for Andy Clarke as he brushes aside the Wimbledon player in the bruising FA Cup clash at Anfield. Razor revelled in the clash, even though the game finished goalless.

Liverpool were supercharged at Hillsborough on 25 February. Despite Des Walker's sterling efforts *(right)* to keep the Reds at bay, a superb strike from Rocket Man, Steve McManaman *(below)*, proved to be a match winner. Three days later, the Reds would end Wimbledon's FA Cup resistance with Ian Rush starring as the Reds' delighted record-breaker *(far top right)*.

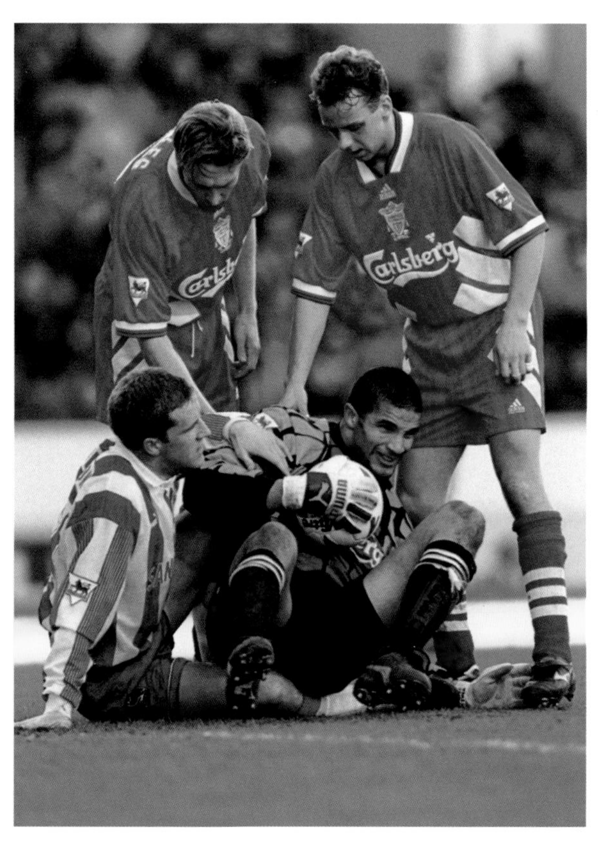
Carlsberg

Lucozade

Carlsberg

Carlsberg

# MARCH '95

## RUSHING TOWARDS ANOTHER DAY OF WEMBLEY GLORY

AS THE Coca-Cola Cup semi-final second leg clash against Crystal Palace got ever closer, skipper Ian Rush declared how much it would mean to him to land a major trophy. He said: *"Even if I am not at Liverpool next season, I'd take so much pleasure in helping the club get back into Europe."*

The Welshman produced a captain's performance to inspire a 2-0 home victory over high-riding Newcastle United. The Reds turned on the style as second half goals from Robbie Fowler and Rush brought a victory that kept the club in the hunt for domestic honours on three fronts.

Liverpool had lost just once in 23 games as they prepared for their midweek semi-final return at Palace. Once again, young Fowler was the goal hero, adding to his decisive first leg strike to earn the Reds a Final date with Bolton Wanderers.

Roared on by their own fans, Palace produced a spell of power play early on. But Fowler latched onto a Jamie Redknapp pass after 27 minutes to fire home a low, angled opener. Liverpool also survived a penalty appeal when Chris Coleman's shot struck John Scales.

Liverpool held on. And after the final whistle had been blown, Roy Evans said: *"The players have worked so hard. They deserve to go to Wembley and win the Cup."* Neil Ruddock added: *"I signed for Liverpool to play at Wembley and win things. I'm happy part of this has come true."*

It was all go for the Merseysiders. Tottenham arrived at Anfield for an FA Cup sixth round game. Unhappily, German superstar, Jurgen Klinsmann, struck a dramatic late winner as Spurs came from behind to deprive Liverpool of two possible Wembley appearances. Robbie Fowler opened the scoring after 38 minutes before Teddy Sheringham curled a magnificent equaliser past David James. Two minutes from time, Klinsmann claimed Sheringham's pass in the area to hit his sensational winner.

It was back to Premiership action with a home game against Coventry City. But hopes of a quick pick-me-up following the Spurs defeat were wrecked by Zimbabwean international, Peter Ndlovu. He took the plaudits after scoring in the 21st, 36th and 85th minutes. In between, Jan Molby pulled one back from the spot and former Anfield defender, David Burrows, scored a late own goal. But a 3-2 reversal was not the best way to prepare for a home game against Manchester United.

The men from Old Trafford had put nine goals past Ipswich Town only 11 days before the teams met at Anfield. And Molby warned: ""*If we play the way we did against Coventry, they could do to us what they did to Ipswich!"* It was simply Jan's way of saying: *"Buck up, or else!"*

The good news was that John Barnes and Phil Babb were ready to return after injury. They helped Liverpool get back on track in a big way. Liverpool beat great rivals United 2-0 in front of a delighted Kop. After 24 minutes, Jamie Redknapp collected Robbie Fowler's square pass to dummy past Paul Ince and Denis Irwin before coolly firing home the opener. Home defender Mark Wright, making his first appearance of the season, had prepared himself for a rough ride against United's lethal front line. But the onslaught never came.

In the end, Steve McManaman's mis-timed shot after 88 minutes deflected off Steve Bruce and sealed a very welcome victory.

Redknapp would now win his first call-up to the full England squad. He was one of five Kop stars in Terry Venables's party for the friendly against Uruguay on 29 March, a game that was taking place just four days before the Coca-Cola Cup Final. McManaman, Jones, Barnes and Ruddock were the other Reds in the squad.

Roy Evans looked to the future by splashing out £2m for Millwall's highly-rated Republic of Ireland winger, Mark Kennedy, who became the country's most expensive 18-year-old. Kennedy revealed: *"I have been a Liverpool fan all my life. My dad is a Liverpool fanatic and he has been over from Ireland many times to watch the team.*

*"Next time he comes, hopefully he will see me play. I am a big fan of Ian Rush. I have a few of his videos and it was a bit of a shock to meet him."*

Kennedy actually thought he would be joining Blackburn Rovers, but Liverpool's stealth paid off as they beat former boss, Kenny Dalglish, to the punch.

The final game of the month took the Reds to White Hart Lane, where they attempted to put behind them the memory of the recent FA Cup defeat at the hands of the north Londoners. David James was in tremendous form in a game that ended 0-0. A 72nd minute penalty save from Jurgen Klinsmann, after Ruddock was adjudged to have fouled the German, capped a marvellous performance by the Liverpool 'keeper.

Striker Lee Jones and midfielder Phil Charnock accepted two-year extensions to their contracts as the Reds continued to look to the future. Charnock's claim to fame was that he became the youngest player to appear in a European game when, at the age of 17 years and seven months, he came on at Anfield as a substitute against Apollon Limassol of Cyprus on 16 September 1992. Prior to this, Jamie Redknapp had held the record.

*"I value the record and the experience from that night, but I am more concerned with the future,"* said Charnock, one of a host of up-and-coming players being groomed in the reserves.

For the present, Rob Jones and John Barnes made the England starting line-up against Uruguay. But the Wembley game that really mattered was now in everyone's sights – the April Coca-Cola Cup showdown with Bolton. The prize for the winner would be a place in Europe.

Ian Rush *(above)* celebrates Robbie Fowler's opening strike in the Geordie joust with Newcastle at Anfield. But the smiles soon disappeared when the world class qualities of Tottenham ace Jurgen Klinsmann *(right)* crushed Liverpool's FA Cup ambitions.

An elated Jamie Redknapp looks forward to a date at Wembley following the Coca-Cola Cup semi-final defeat of Crystal Palace. After a hard campaign, Liverpool were on the verge of more Cup glory.

Hitman Robbie Fowler holds his hands in the air *(above, right)* after scoring the decisive goal against Palace that confirmed Liverpool's Wembley return. Indeed, the defeat of Palace meant a lot to the entire Liverpool team.

England Under 21 star Jamie Redknapp's 24th minute opener had United in a spin *(left)*. The visitors conceded a late own goal as their title tilt nose-dived *(below)*.

Rivals Manchester United suffered a severe title set-back at Anfield on 19 March. It was a day when total commitment was the name of the game, with Ian Rush *(above)* and Neil Ruddock *(above, right)* prepared to give the Reds' cause everything.

Steve McManaman was the Liverpool goalscorer in a hard-fought game at Manchester City in mid-April. The Reds lost 2-1, despite McManaman doing his best to inflict further damage on City's defence.

# APRIL '95

## ENJOYING LIFE IN THE FAST LANE

ALL OF THE hard work put in by the manager, coaching staff and players was about to pay dividends. And with the Coca-Cola Cup Final now just a matter of hours away, defender John Scales had just one regret. *"I just wish I had come to Anfield sooner,"* he said.

The former Wimbledon star had yearned for a move to a big club. Liverpool had provided him with exactly the right challenge and here he was, on the brink of Wembley glory. *"I'd definitely have liked to have come here sooner. But it's better late than never,"* he mused. *"My contract at Wimbledon would have been up this summer and maybe I would have moved on anyway. But I'm pleased I was able to come to Liverpool this season. It had been no secret that I wanted to join them. I felt this was the club which would best suit me and that I would suit the club. I think that has been proved."*

Scales was clearly delighted with his new team-mates. He said: *"There are some of the best players in the country at Anfield. Any player – past or present – will tell you that if you are with great players you will play better. We have a good blend with youngsters like Robbie Fowler, Steve McManaman and Jamie Redknapp. I've not seen young players like that anywhere else."*

Looking forward, Scales added: *"Playing football at the top level is about getting to cup finals and winning trophies. When you are in your twenties, you think you are going to be back at Wembley every couple of years because you have your whole career ahead of you. But in reality it's different. It's a bit of a cliché to say you want to win the League and everything else. But the Premiership title is the biggest honour in domestic football and that's what everyone strives for."*

Wembley's Twin Towers now beckoned. And no one was going to stop Roy Evans and his team from putting another piece of silverware in the famous Anfield trophy room. The Coca-Cola Cup success over Bolton, featured in the opening chapter, was a clear signal to English soccer that Liverpool were back in a big way.

Jan Molby was now offered a new contract. As the stylish Danish midfielder considered it, he said: *"My last couple of years may not have been as fruitful as my earlier ones, but I can only have fond memories of Liverpool."*

The Reds had an early opportunity to parade their newly won trophy when Southampton arrived for a game that was crucial to the visitors' Premiership future. Former Liverpool 'keeper, Bruce Grobbelaar, was in the Saints' line-up and looking forward to an interesting night in front of the Kop.

Roy Evans was happy to see his players parade the Cup before the kick-off, but he was more interested in securing three points. *"First and foremost, we owe it to our supporters to win,"* he said. *"We are only interested in what Liverpool FC stands for and we've stressed that we want to finish in a higher League position."*

The players responded superbly to the manager's words with a 3-1 victory, in which Ian Rush grabbed a double and Robbie Fowler also got in on the act. But the elation at the result was dampened by a bad injury to Stig Inge Bjornebye who broke his leg.

The defender faced a five-week spell in plaster, but he was determined to be positive, saying: *"I don't really want to complain because people have suffered horrible injuries in football. Mine is disappointing because it means I can't complete the season, but I won't be out for too long. I'm going to do some really hard work over the summer to get fit."*

Liverpool now faced up to a hectic four games in nine days. On 9 April, the Reds lost 1-0 at home to Leeds. The 37,454 fans at Anfield were disappointed, but hopeful that the players could put things right at Arsenal three days later. Typically, the side bounced right back and a Robbie Fowler goal was good enough to secure the points.

On 14 April, a Steve McManaman goal could not prevent a 2-1 reversal at Manchester City. But the roller coaster spell took off again with a 2-0 home success over Leicester, with those irrepressible partners – Rush and Fowler – securing the points. It was a match in which Steve Harkness had an opportunity to demonstrate what he could do. He marked only his third Premiership outing with a faultless display. *"I expected to have left Anfield a long time ago,"* he said afterwards. *"But I'm still here and battling away."*

It was suggested that Glasgow Rangers, crowned Scottish Champions for the seventh successive year, would make a renewed attempt to sign Neil Ruddock. Boss Evans nipped the speculation in the bud straight away, declaring: *"There is no chance of Ruddock going. He is not for sale."*

Evans was keen to strengthen, not weaken his squad. He said he would have no hesitation in buying any player who fitted the bill. *"The priority, because of the European situation, has to be English players," said Roy. "But I wouldn't have any worries about signing a foreigner if we considered him to be outstanding."*

The boss had already paid out £10m for Phil Babb, John Scales and Mark Kennedy. *"I can't control the prices,"* he said. *"But if I feel someone is the right player, I'm not afraid to buy big."*

Was a certain Stan Collymore in the manager's mind as he uttered those words? The Forest star was certainly a priority target. With new players on his mind, Evans ran the rule over Portuguese striker, Joao Pinto, without following up his interest.

The month ended with a 2-1 away win at Norwich which spelled doom for the East Anglian side. Harkness and Rush were the scorers. It had been a busy and fruitful spell, topped by that Coca-Cola triumph and the certainty that Liverpool were back in Europe, come what may. And, there was still a mighty finale to come against Blackburn Rovers.

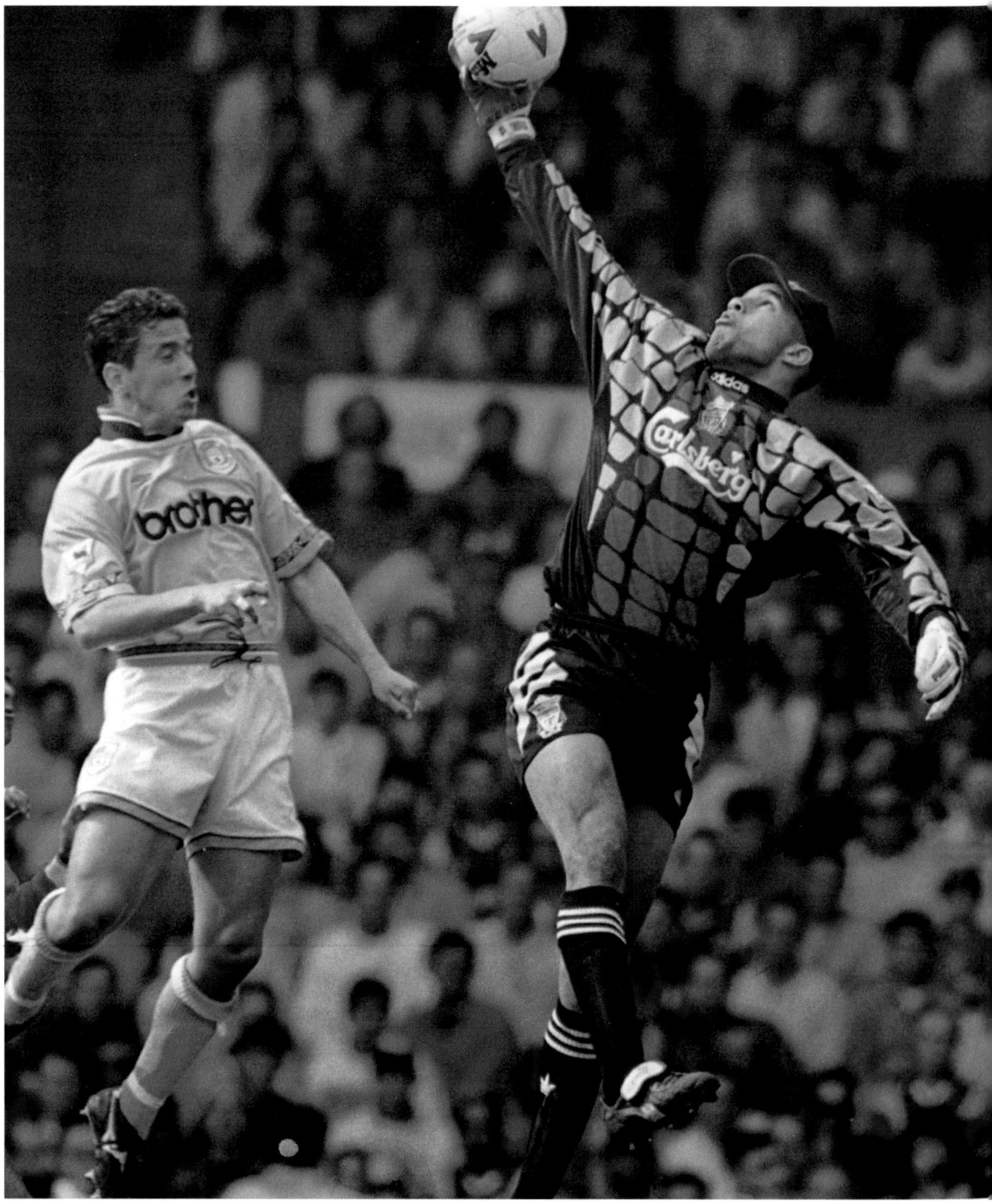

Michael Thomas sees an opening against Manchester City *(above, left)*, while 'keeper David James *(above)* rises high to thwart another City attack.

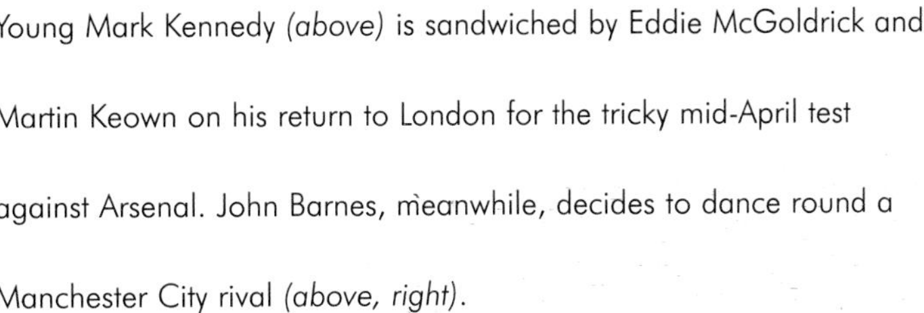

Young Mark Kennedy *(above)* is sandwiched by Eddie McGoldrick and Martin Keown on his return to London for the tricky mid-April test against Arsenal. John Barnes, meanwhile, decides to dance round a Manchester City rival *(above, right)*.

Mitre

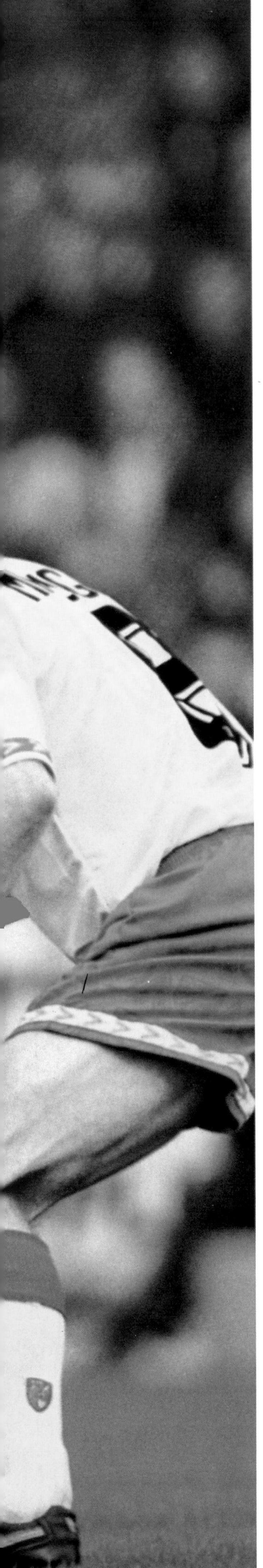

Steve McManaman prepares to take on two defenders during the clash against struggling Norwich at Carrow Road *(left)*. Mark Kennedy *(above)* brushes aside the challenge of Leicester's Mark Blake at Anfield. And the winger and Robbie Fowler congratulate Steve McManaman following Macca's goal against Manchester City *(top)*.

# MAY '95

## LOOKING FOR THE PERFECT FINALE

THE MERRY month of May is traditionally one of fun. So when a Liverpool player said he had enrolled on a refereeing course with a view to eventually taking up the whistle, a few eyebrows were raised. But Nigel Clough was deadly serious. He was one of 16 professionals who took up the initiative handed by Gordon Taylor, chief executive of the Professional Footballers' Association.

*"I've put my name down. There are a lot of ex-players out of work. I think this is an ideal way for players to put something back into football because not everyone wants to go into coaching,"* said Clough.

Liverpool began the final month of the season with a game at Wimbledon. The goalless draw marked the start of an undistinguished three match spell. A magnificent 40,154 crowd in the Midlands saw Aston Villa claim a 2-0 home victory and three crucial points in their battle to stay in the top flight. An even more emphatic defeat was to follow in London at Upton Park, where West Ham romped home 3-0.

But the Reds would now be involved in the perfect finale – a home game against Blackburn Rovers that would decide the Championship. There was a school of thought outside Merseyside that said Liverpool would step aside and allow their former manager, Kenny Dalglish, a clean run to a sensational title success with Rovers, at the expense of great rivals Manchester United.

It was such an outrageous suggestion. And Roy Evans couldn't help but pick up on it after a goals from John Barnes and Jamie Redknapp secured a 2-1 victory for the Reds, a result that was immaterial in the end because of United's own failure to win at West Ham. *"There was a lot of hype about what we were going to do, said Evans. "I wasn't happy with what was printed before this match. We played our part in the game and I don't know if anyone wants to give us any more stick.*

*"Kenny Dalglish is a friend of mine, but I've also got friends in Manchester. It's sad for United, but Blackburn got more points, deserved to win the title and I congratulate them."*

Blackburn chairman, Robert Coar, now paid Liverpool and their fans a remarkable tribute. He said: *"I wish to place on record our appreciation of the way Liverpool fans conducted themselves and of their contribution to what was, for us, a memorable final day of the 1994/95 season.*

*"Naturally we would have liked to have clinched the title at home, but the response of all Liverpool supporters to our success was magnificent. The way they responded made it a day no-one will forget. They were a credit to their club, the game of football and themselves."*

Liverpool had every right to feel proud of their own contribution in that last-gasp title decider. But more than that, the club had every right to feel delighted with its achievements in a season of revival.

The rebirth of the Reds thrilled everyone at Anfield and sent out a message to the whole of football that Liverpool Football Club was back on track for glory.

Blackburn's £5m striker Chris Sutton immediately picked up on it when he named Liverpool as the leading pretenders to Blackburn's newly won Premiership crown. He said: *"Liverpool are a hell of a side. Robbie Fowler bangs in the goals and they knock the ball about well. They beat us with a superb free-kick. I'm sure they are going to be challenging for the title next season after winning the Coca-Cola Cup this year.*

*"With a bit more consistency they will be stronger. You can never say for sure if anyone is going to win something, but I definitely think Liverpool will be up there. As for Robbie Fowler, he thoroughly deserved to be named Young Player of the Year."*

David James, the Reds' outstanding 'keeper, reflected on a memorable campaign. He said: *"If we'd done the right things throughout the season, it could have been us celebrating instead of Blackburn.*

*"I really want that to happen, but you have to put it in perspective. In the League, we hadn't done a lot in the last three years. So to expect us to turn round this season and win the Championship was a bit much.*

*"This has been a stepping stone. We've finished fourth which is better than last year and the year before, so there is improvement. There's no reason why we should not be challenging next season if we apply ourselves correctly."*

This optimism would soon be increased when Roy Evans made a bold summer move for Stan Collymore, paying Nottingham Forest a British record £8.5m fee for the England striker. Evans beat off a strong challenge from arch-rivals Everton to secure the player's signature. The magnitude of the deal highlighted the Reds' determination to set themselves up for a powerful tilt at the 1995/96 campaign. What a season it promises to be.

Collymore's strength, pace and goal potential had added to an armoury that is already impressive by anyone's standards. Liverpool are building for the future in a big way with an array of talented and ambitious young professionals.

With Europe in mind, Liverpool accept that they must build a squad around a solid base of English players.

Collymore, Jamie Redknapp, Rob Jones, David James, John Scales, Neil Ruddock, John Barnes, Steve McManaman and Robbie Fowler – to name but nine – will all be knocking of England manager Terry Venables' door in the months ahead with a view to pressing the European Championship claims.

Liverpool boss Roy Evans knows that before any one of these players can fulfil their international ambitions, they must first produce the goods for him in a Liverpool shirt.

Competition for places will be fierce – but that is what makes a good team great.

Carlsber

Blackburn's David Batty is always a tough opponent, but Jamie Redknapp *(above, right)* had the measure of the Rovers' star as the season drew to its climax on a winning note for the Reds. Robbie Fowler *(above left)*, meanwhile, is unable to hide a smile despite the intensity of Premiership battle.

Liverpool players line up to keep their opponents at bay *(top)* while Steve McManaman *(above)* was soon testing Rovers at the other end. The imposing figure of David James *(right)* ends this West Ham attack with Trevor Morley unable to cash in.

Blackburn's Tim Sherwood found John Barnes *(above, left)* a real handful as the season drew to a magnificent close at Anfield. Similar determination is shown by Dominic Matteo *(above, right)* against Villa's Gary Charles.

John Barnes *(above)* lashes home a tremendous opener which threatens to destroy Blackburn's chances of lifting the title. The Reds won a superb game 2-1 – but Rovers still snatched the Championship.

Coca-Cola

# STEVE McMANAMAN

## THE BOY WITH STARDUST ON HIS BOOTS

STEVE McMANAMAN talks like he's the boy from next door. The likeable Liverpudlian is as down to earth as they come. But he was born to be a soccer superstar. You cannot coach the kind of skills he displays, week in, week out in front of the adoring Kop. Leaving defenders trailing in his wake is an ability that comes naturally to the young winger who has just enjoyed a truly remarkable year.

He is the current Merseyside Footballer of the Year, voted into first place ahead of a string of talented soccer rivals by the readers of the Liverpool Echo. He also picked up the Merseyside Sports Personality of the Year award, which shows that he is respected on a much wider spectrum.

His achievements on the home front finally received international recognition when he won his first full England cap. And a remarkable spell of personal success reached a fitting climax when he scored both of the goals that won Liverpool the Coca-Cola Cup at Wembley.

McManaman is heading for the very top of his profession. Almost inevitably, people compare him with Manchester United's supremely talented Welsh winger, Ryan Giggs. Merseysiders believe that Giggs should look on this as the ultimate tribute!

The Reds and England ace shrugs aside this healthy competition between two high profile individuals, saying: *"I'm just quite happy to stay out of the limelight and do my own thing. People have compared Ryan with George Best because of the Manchester United connection. And he has been doing television adverts and all that stuff.*

*"But I'm fine. I'm more than happy to keep low profile. Money is not my goal. I'm not being funny. It's just that I'm a low key person. I'm from a working class background. Okay, I'm well paid now and that's fine. I'm more than happy to stay at Anfield, keep playing, keep winning things and staying low profile."*

When McManaman gets the ball at his feet, he spins and twists and turns defenders inside out. McManaman becomes Supermac. Without a doubt, he is one of the most exciting talents in the country. But he chooses to keep his feet firmly on the ground.

*"People say I have been playing well. So long as that's the view of the Liverpool fans, I'm happy,"* he says. *"You take notice of the people you admire. I always listen to my dad. If he says I played badly, I generally know it's true. If he says I played well, then I know I played well. I also listen to the staff at Anfield. As for the people who just shout willy nilly, well, that's another thing."*

Perhaps it was his first season in a Liverpool shirt that taught McManaman that football can be a real roller coaster ride. He had his critics early on. But that was all part of the learning curve. He said: *"I can't explain the difference between the season just gone and the previous one. Who can tell? I'm exactly the same person. I've been training every day, but I couldn't say I practiced and practiced or anything. Maybe I'm a different person on the pitch. I think my role has definitely got something to do with it."*

Manager Roy Evans has been prepared to give McManaman the freedom of the park. And the youngster has revelled with this extra freedom. Steve believes the spirit at Anfield has never been higher: *"I think there is more camaraderie between the lads. We are playing with a lot more confidence."*

On a personal note, he naturally wants to further his claim for a regular England place. He said: *"Playing for England means a lot to me. I captained the Under-21s which was also a great personal honour."*

The skillful Reds' winger believes Liverpool can build on the tremendous base that was season 1994/95. *"I thoroughly enjoyed my first season in professional football. But finishing fourth this time out and winning the Coca-Cola Cup was a real achievement. The average age of our team is quite low, so we should be able to move forward with confidence."*

# 1994

# 1995

Date: **August 20th, 1994**
Venue: **Selhurst Park 18,084**
Tournament: **Carling Premiership**
Referee: **R. Hart**

**Crystal Palace - (0) 1**
Armstrong (49)
Martyn, Pitcher, Young, Coleman, Gordon, Salako, Southgate, Wilkins, Rodger, Armstrong, Preece
**Subs:** Dyer (for Preece 24), Bowry (for Wilkins 82), Wilmot not used

**Liverpool - (3) 6**
Molby pen (12), McManaman (14, 76), Fowler (45), Rush (60, 74)
James, R. Jones, Nicol, Ruddock, Bjornebye, McManaman, Redknapp, Molby, Barnes, Rush, Fowler.
**Subs:** Thomas (Molby 86). Harkness and Stensgaard not used.

| Pos | P | W | D | L | F | Ag | Pts |
|---|---|---|---|---|---|---|---|
| 1 | 1 | 1 | 0 | 0 | 6 | 1 | 3 |

Date: **August 28, 1994**
Venue: **Anfield 30,017**
Tournament: **Carling Premiership**
Referee: **Alan Wilkie**

**Liverpool - (3) 3**
Fowler (26, 29, 31)
James, R. Jones, Nicol, Ruddock, Bjornebye, McManaman, Redknapp, Molby, Barnes, Fowler, Rush.
**Subs:** Thomas (for Molby 57). Matteo and Stensgaard not used.

**Arsenal - (0) 0**
Seaman, Dixon, Winterburn, Adams, Keown, Schwarz, Jensen, Campbell, Wright, Smith, Merson.
**Subs:** Davis (for Jensen 73), Linighan (for Merson 73). Barton not used.

| Pos | P | W | D | L | F | Ag | Pts |
|---|---|---|---|---|---|---|---|
| 5 | 2 | 2 | 0 | 0 | 9 | 1 | 6 |

Date: **August 31, 1994**
Venue: **The Dell 15,190**
Tournament: **Carling Premiership**
Referee: **M. Bodenham**

**Southampton (0) 0**
Grobbelaar, Kenna, Benali, Monkou, Charlton, Allen, Magilton, Madison, Heaney, Le Tissier, Banger.
**Subs:** Hall (for Monkou 41), Widdrington and Beasant not used.

**Liverpool - (1) 2**
Fowler( 21), Barnes (77)
James, R.Jones, Nicol, Ruddock, Bjornebye, McManaman, Redknapp, Molby, Barnes, Rush, Fowler.
**Subs:** Clough, Harkness and Stensgaard not used.

| Pos | P | W | D | L | F | Ag | Pts |
|---|---|---|---|---|---|---|---|
| 4 | 3 | 3 | 0 | 0 | 11 | 1 | 9 |

Date: **September 10th, 1994**
Venue: **Anfield 30,907**
Tournament: **Carling Premiership**
Referee: **P. Dansen**

**Liverpool - (0) 0**
James, R. Jones, Scales, Ruddock, Bjornebye, McManaman, Redknapp, Molby, Barnes, Rush, Fowler.
**Subs:** Stensgaard, Babb and Clough not used.

**West Ham United - (0) 0**
Miklosko, Breacker, Roland, Potts, Martin, Allen, Butler, Moncur, Rush, Marsh, Cottee.
**Subs:** Chapman, Whitbread and Feuer not used.

| Pos | P | W | D | L | F | Ag | Pts |
|---|---|---|---|---|---|---|---|
| 4 | 4 | 3 | 1 | 0 | 11 | 1 | 10 |

Date: **September 17th**
Venue: **Old Trafford 43,740**
Tournament: **Carling Premiership**
Referee: **K. Morton**

**Manchester United - (0) 2**
Kanchelskis (71), McClair (73).
Schmeichel, May, Irwin, Bruce, Pallister, Kanchelskis, Cantona, Ince, Sharp, Hughes, Giggs.
**Subs:** McClair (for Hughes 59), Butt and Pilkington not used.

**Liverpool - (0) 0**
James, Jones, Bjornebye, Scales, Ruddock, Molby, Redknapp, McManaman, Rush, Barnes, Fowler.
**Subs:** Babb (for Molby 70), Clough and Stensgaard not used.

| Pos | P | W | D | L | F | Ag | Pts |
|---|---|---|---|---|---|---|---|
| 5 | 5 | 3 | 1 | 1 | 11 | 3 | 10 |

Date: **September 24, 1994**
Venue: **St. James' Park 34,435**
Tournament: **Carling Premiership**
Referee: **P. Don**

**Newcastle - (0) 1**
Lee (50)
Srnicek, Hottiger, Beresford, Venison, Peacock, Albert, Lee, Beardsley, Sellars, Fox, Cole.
**Subs:** Howey (for Venison 23), Watson (for Sellars (83), Hooper not used.

**Liverpool - (0)1**
Rush (70)
James, R. Jones, Scales, Ruddock, Babb, Bjornebye, McManaman, Molby, Barnes, Fowler, Rush.
**Subs:** Clough (for Rush 90), Redknapp and Stensgaard not used.

| Pos | P | W | D | L | F | Ag | Pts |
|---|---|---|---|---|---|---|---|
| 6 | 6 | 3 | 2 | 1 | 12 | 4 | 11 |

Date: **October 1st, 1994**
Venue: **Anfield 31,493**
Tournament: **Carling Premiership**
Referee: **G. Willard**

**Liverpool - (0) 4**
Rush (51), McManaman (54, 86), Walker og (66)
James, R. Jones, Nicol, Ruddock, Babb, Bjornebye, McManaman, Molby, Barnes, Fowler, Rush.
**Subs:** Redknapp (for Fowler 76). Stensgaard and Clough not used

**Sheffield Wednesday - (1) 1**
Nolan (33)
Pressman, Atherton, Nolan, Petrescu, Walker, Hyde, Bart Williams, Sheridan, Sinton, Bright, Watson.
**Subs:** Hirst (for Watson 58), Pearce and Key not used

| Pos | P | W | D | L | F | Ag | Pts |
|---|---|---|---|---|---|---|---|
| 5 | 7 | 4 | 2 | 1 | 16 | 5 | 14 |

Date: **October 8th, 1994.**
Venue: **Anfield 32,158**
Tournament: **Carling Premiership**
Referee: **K. Burge**

**Liverpool - (2) 3**
Ruddock (20), Fowler (26, 57)
James, Scales, Ruddock, Babb, R. Jones, McManaman, Molby, Barnes, Bjornebye, Rush, Fowler.
**Subs:** Redknapp (for Rush 79). Stensgaard and Clough not used.

**Aston Villa - (1) 2**
Whittingham (37), Staunton (90)
Bosnich, Barrett, Staunton, McGrath, Ehiogu, Houghton, Townsend, Parker, Yorke, Saunders, Whittingham.
**Subs:** Lamptey (for Houghton 72), King (for Townsend 31), Spink not used.

| Pos | P | W | D | L | F | Ag | Pts |
|---|---|---|---|---|---|---|---|
| 4 | 8 | 5 | 2 | 1 | 19 | 7 | 17 |

Date: **October 15th, 1994**
Venue: **Ewood Park 30,263**
Tournament: **Carling Premiership**
Referee: **Brian Hill**

**Blackburn - (0) 3**
Atkins (52, Sutton (57, 72)
Flowers, Berg, Le Saux, Gayle, Hendry, Wilcox, Atkins, Warhurst, Ripley, Shearer, Sutton.
**Subs:** Slater, Pearce and Mimms not used.

**Liverpool - (1) 2**
Fowler (29), Barnes (59)
James, Scales, Ruddock, Babb, R. Jones, McManaman, Molby, Barnes, Bjornebye, Rush, Fowler.
**Subs:** Redknapp (for Bjornebye 78), Clough and Stensgaard not used.

| Pos | P | W | D | L | F | Ag | Pts |
|---|---|---|---|---|---|---|---|
| 5 | 9 | 5 | 2 | 2 | 21 | 10 | 17 |

Date: **October 22nd, 1994**
Venue: **Anfield 31,139**
Tournament: **Carling Premiership**
Referee: **P. Jones**

**Liverpool - (2) 3**
McManaman (20), Fowler (35), Barnes (63)
James, Scales, Ruddock, Babb, R. Jones, McManaman, Redknapp, Barnes, Bjornebye, Rush, Fowler.
**Subs:** Clough (for Rush 81), L. Jones (for Fowler 81). Stensgaard not used.

**Wimbledon - (0) 0**
Segers, Barton, Fitzgerald, Elkins, Reeves, Joseph, Gayle, Perry, Fear, Ardley, Ekoku.
**Subs:** Blissett (for Perry 46), Castledine (for Gayle 73), Murphy not used.

| Pos | P | W | D | L | F | Ag | Pts |
|---|---|---|---|---|---|---|---|
| 5 | 10 | 6 | 2 | 2 | 24 | 10 | 20 |

Date: **October 29th, 1994**
Venue: **Portman Road 22,513**
Tournament: **Carling Premiership**
Referee: **Paul Durkin**

**Ipswich Town - (0) 1**
Paz (65).
Forrest, Stockwell, Youds, Sedgley, Vaughan, Thompson, Williams, Palmer, Johnson, Paz, Guentchev.
**Subs:** Linighan, (for Palmer 76), Yallop and Baker not used.

**Liverpool - (1) 3**
Barnes (39), Fowler (56, 59)
James, Scales, Ruddock, Babb, R. Jones, McManaman, Redknapp, Barnes, Bjornebye, Rush, Fowler.
**Subs:** Clough, Molby and Stensgaard not used

| Pos | P | W | D | L | F | Ag | Pts |
|---|---|---|---|---|---|---|---|
| 5 | 11 | 7 | 2 | 2 | 27 | 11 | 23 |

Date: **October 31st, 1994**
Venue: **Loftus Road 18,295**
Tournament: **Carling Premiership**
Referee: **Terry Holbrook**

**QPR - (1) 2**
Sinclair (28), Ferdinand (85).
Dykstra, Bardsley, Wilson, Yates, McDonald, Impey, Barker, Hodge, Sinclair, Ferdinand, Gallen.
**Subs:** Maddix, Dichio, Roberts not used.

**Liverpool - (0) 1**
Barnes (65)
James, Scales, Ruddock, Babb, R. Jones, McManaman, Redknapp, Barnes, Bjornebye, Rush, Fowler.
**Subs:** Molby (for Babb 68), Stensgaard and Clough.

| Pos | P | W | D | L | F | Ag | Pts |
|---|---|---|---|---|---|---|---|
| 5 | 12 | 7 | 2 | 3 | 28 | 13 | 23 |

Date: **November 5th , 1994**
Venue: **Anfield 33,329**
Tournament: **Carling Premiership**
Referee: **Joe Worrall**

**Liverpool - (1) 1**
Fowler (14)
James, Scales, Ruddock, Babb, R. Jones, McManaman, Redknapp, Barnes, Bjornebye, Rush, Fowler
**Subs:** Molby (for Scales 29). Stensgaard and Clough not used.

**Nottingham Forest - (0) 0**
Crossley, Little, Pearce, Cooper, Chettle, Phillips, Bohinen, Stone, Woan, Lee, Roy.
**Subs:** Gemmill, Black and Wright not used.

| Pos | P | W | D | L | F | Ag | Pts |
|---|---|---|---|---|---|---|---|
| **5** | **13** | **8** | **2** | **3** | **30** | **13** | **26** |

Date: **November 9th , 1994**
Venue: **Anfield 32,855**
Tournament: **Carling Premiership**
Referee: **Graham Poll**

**Liverpool - (3) 3**
Fowler (9, 10), Ruddock (25)
James, Molby, Ruddock, Babb, R. Jones, McManaman, Redknapp, Barnes, Bjornebye, Rush, Fowler.
**Subs:** Clough, Stensgaard and L. Jones not used

**Chelsea - (1) 1**
Spencer (3)
Hitchcock, Barnes, Myers, Kjeldbjerg, Johnson, Rocastle, Newton, Spackman, Wise, Shipperley, Spencer,
**Subs:** Burley (for Shipperley 74), Hopkin (for Rocastle 45), Judge not used.

| Pos | P | W | D | L | F | Ag | Pts |
|---|---|---|---|---|---|---|---|
| **4** | **14** | **9** | **2** | **3** | **33** | **14** | **29** |

Date: **November 21st, 1994**
Venue: **Goodison Park 39,866**
Tournament: **Carling Premiership**
Referee: **Dermot Gallagher**

**Everton - (0) 2**
Ferguson (57), Rideout (89).
Southall, Jackson, Ablett, Watson, Unsworth, Horne, Parkinson, Ebbrell, Hinchcliffe, Amokachi, Ferguson.
**Subs:** Rideout (for Jackson 45), Limpar (for Amokachi 74), Kearton not used.

**Liverpool - (0) 0**
James, R. Jones, Bjornebye, Babb, Ruddock, Scales, McManaman, Molby, Barnes, Fowler, Rush.
**Subs:** Redknapp (for Bjornebye 63). Clough and Stensgaard not used.

| Pos | P | W | D | L | F | Ag | Pts |
|---|---|---|---|---|---|---|---|
| **4** | **15** | **9** | **2** | **4** | **32** | **16** | **29** |

Date: **November 26th, 1994**
Venue: **Anfield 35,007**
Tournament: **Carling Premiership**
Referee: **Stephen Lodge**

**Liverpool - (1) 1**
Fowler pen (39)
James, Scales, Ruddock, Babb, R. Jones, McManaman, Redknapp, Barnes, Bjornebye, Rush, Fowler
**Subs:** Thomas (for Barnes 55). L. Jones and Stensgaard not used.

**Tottenham - (0) 1**
Ruddock og (78)
Walker, Austin, Campbell, Calderwood, Mabbutt, Howells, Barmby, Popescu, Anderton, Sheringham, Klinsmann.
**Subs:** Dumitrescu (for Anderton 45), Scott and Day not used.

| Pos | P | W | D | L | F | Ag | Pts |
|---|---|---|---|---|---|---|---|
| **4** | **16** | **9** | **3** | **4** | **33** | **17** | **30** |

Date: **December 3rd, 1994**
Venue: **Highfield Road 21,029**
Tournament: **Carling Premiership**
Referee: **Keith Burge**

**Coventry - (0) 1**
Flynn (57)
Ogrizovic, Borrows, Morgan, Pressley, Busst, Darby, Flynn, Ndlovu, Cook, Jenkinson, Jones.
**Subs:** Pickering (for Busst 45), Sheridan and Gould not used.

**Liverpool - (1) 1**
Rush (2)
James, Scales, Ruddock, Babb, Harkness, McManaman, Redknapp, Thomas, Bjornebye, Rush, Fowler
**Subs:** Walters (for Bjornebye 79). Prudhoe and Clough not used.

| Pos | P | W | D | L | F | Ag | Pts |
|---|---|---|---|---|---|---|---|
| **4** | **17** | **9** | **4** | **4** | **34** | **18** | **31** |

Date: **December 11th, 1994**
Venue: **Anfield 30,972**
Tournament: **Carling Premiership**
Referee: **Kelvin Morton**

**Liverpool - (0) 0**
James, Harkness, Scales, Ruddock, Babb, Bjornebye, Redknapp, Barnes, Thomas, Clough, Fowler.
**Subs:** Walters (for Bjornebye 45). Matteo and Prudhoe not used.

**Crystal Palace - (0) 0**
Martyn, Humphrey, Shaw, Southgate, Gordon, Bowry, Pitcher, Newman, Salako, Armstrong, Preece.
**Subs:** Dyer, Matthew, Wilmot

| Pos | P | W | D | L | F | Ag | Pts |
|---|---|---|---|---|---|---|---|
| **4** | **18** | **9** | **5** | **4** | **34** | **18** | **32** |

Date: **December 18th, 1994**
Venue: **Stamford Bridge 27,050**
Tournament: **Carling Premiership**
Referee: **Dermot Gallagher**

**Chelsea - (0) 0**
Kharin, Newton, Minto, Johnson, Sinclair, Rocastle, Wise, Spackman, Hoddle, Peacock, Furlong.
**Subs:** Stein (for Rocastle 70), Barness and Hitchcock not used.

**Liverpool - (0) 0**
James, Thomas, Scales, Ruddock, Babb, Bjornebye, Redknapp, Barnes, Walters, Rush, Fowler
**Subs:** Harkness, Clough and Prudhoe not used.

| Pos | P | W | D | L | F | Ag | Pts |
|---|---|---|---|---|---|---|---|
| **5** | **19** | **9** | **6** | **4** | **34** | **18** | **33** |

Date: **December 26th, 1994**
Venue: **Filbert Street 21,393**
Tournament: **Carling Premiership**
Referee: **Gerald Ashby**

**Leicester City - (0) 1**
Roberts (87)
Poole, Grayson, Willis, Hill, Whitlow, Carr, Thompson, Draper, Blake, Philpott, Oldfield.
**Subs:** Agnew (for Carr 71), Roberts (for Thompson 74), Ward not used.

**Liverpool - (0) 2**
Fowler pen (67), Rush (77)
James, Scales, Ruddock, Babb, R. Jones, McManaman, Redknapp, Barnes, Bjornebye, Fowler, Rush.
**Subs:** Thomas (for Jones 87). Walters and Prudhoe not used.

| Pos | P | W | D | L | F | Ag | Pts |
|---|---|---|---|---|---|---|---|
| **4** | **20** | **10** | **6** | **4** | **36** | **19** | **36** |

Date: **December 28th , 1994**
Venue: **Anfield 38,122**
Tournament: **Carling Premiership**
Referee: **Robbie Hart**

**Liverpool - (0) 2**
Phelan og (55), Fowler (82)
James, Scales, Ruddock, Babb, R. Jones, McManaman, Redknapp, Barnes, Bjornebye, Rush, Fowler
**Subs:** Walters, Thomas and Prudhoe not used.

**Manchester City - (0) 0**
Dibble, Lomas, Phelan, Brightwell, Kernaghan, Gaudino, Flitcroft, Beagrie, Summerbee, Walsh, Rosler.
**Subs:** Vonk, (for Brightwell 45), Simpson and Margetson not used.

| Pos | P | W | D | L | F | Ag | Pts |
|---|---|---|---|---|---|---|---|
| **3** | **21** | **11** | **6** | **4** | **38** | **19** | **39** |

Date: **December 31st, 1994**
Venue: **Elland Road 38,563**
Tournament: **Carling Premiership**
Referee: **Alan Wilkie**

**Leeds - (0) 0**
Lukic, Kelly, Dorigo, Wetherall, Pemberton, Radebe, Strachan, McAllister, Speed, Whelan, Masinga.
**Subs:** Whyte (for Strachan 63), Worthington (for Dorigo 61), Beeney not used.

**Liverpool - (1) 2**
Redknapp (18), Fowler (76)
James, R. Jones, Babb, Rush, Barnes, Scales, Redknapp, McManaman, Bjornebye, Fowler, Ruddock
**Subs:** Thomas, Walters and Prudhoe not used

| Pos | P | W | D | L | F | Ag | Pts |
|---|---|---|---|---|---|---|---|
| **3** | **22** | **12** | **6** | **4** | **40** | **19** | **42** |

Date: **January 2nd, 1995**
Venue: **Anfield 34,709**
Tournament: **Carling Premiership**
Referee: **Keith Cooper**

**Liverpool - (2) 4**
Scales (14), Fowler (38, 47), Rush (83)
James, Jones, Bjornebye, Scales, Ruddock, Babb, Redknapp, McManaman, Barnes, Rush, Fowler.
**Subs:** Walters, Thomas and Prudhoe not used.

**Norwich City - (0) 0**
Marshall, Prior, Polston, Newman, Sutch, Goss, Crook, Milligan, Ullathorne, Sheron, Ward.
**Subs:** Adams (for Goss 45), Eadie (for Newman 45), Crowfoot not used.

| Pos | P | W | D | L | F | Ag | Pts |
|---|---|---|---|---|---|---|---|
| **3** | **23** | **13** | **6** | **4** | **44** | **19** | **45** |

Date: **January 14, 1995**
Venue: **Anfield 32,733**
Tournament: **Carling Premiership**
Referee: **Roger Gifford**

**Liverpool - (0) 0**
James, Jones, Bjornebye, Scales, Ruddock, Babb, Redknapp, Thomas, McManaman, Rush, Fowler.
**Subs:** Walters (for Bjornebye 56), Nicol and Stensgaard not used.

**Ipswich Town (1) 1**
Tanner (30)
Forrest, Yallop, Johnson, Wark, Linighan, Williams, Sedgley, Thompson, Tanner, Slater, Paz.
**Subs:** Mason, Youds and Baker not used.

| Pos | P | W | D | L | F | Ag | Pts |
|---|---|---|---|---|---|---|---|
| **3** | **24** | **13** | **6** | **5** | **44** | **20** | **45** |

Date: **January 24th, 1995**
Venue: **Anfield 39,505**
Tournament: **Carling Premiership**
Referee: **Brian Hill**

**Liverpool - (0) 0**
James, Jones, Bjornebye, Scales, Ruddock, Babb, Redknapp, McManaman, Barnes, Rush, Fowler.
**Subs:** Walters, Thomas and Stensgaard not used.

**Everton (0) 0**
Southall, Jackson, Burrows, Watson, Unsworth, Horne, Ebbrell, Hinchcliffe, Parkinson, Ferguson, Rideout.
**Subs:** Limpar, Barlow and Reeves not used.

| Pos | P | W | D | L | F | Ag | Pts |
|---|---|---|---|---|---|---|---|
| **3** | **25** | **13** | **7** | **5** | **44** | **20** | **46** |

Date: **February 4th, 1995**
Venue: **City Ground 25,416**
Tournament: **Carling Premiership**
Referee: **Gary Willard**

**Nottingham Forest (1) 1**
Collymore (11)
Crossley, Lytle, Haaland, Cooper, Chettle, Phillips, Stone, Gemmill, Woan, Roy, Collymore.
**Subs:** Lee (for Roy 87), Warner and Filan not used.

**Liverpool - (0) 1**
Fowler (90)
James, Jones, Matteo, Scales, Ruddock, Babb, Redknapp, McManaman, Rush, Barnes, Fowler.
**Subs:** Walters (for Matteo 80), Thomas (for Redknapp 73), Stensgaard not used.

| Pos | P | W | D | L | F | Ag | Pts |
|---|---|---|---|---|---|---|---|
| **4** | **26** | **13** | **8** | **5** | **45** | **21** | **47** |

Date: **February 11th, 1995**
Venue: **Anfield 35,996**
Tournament: **Carling Premiership**
Referee: **Dermot Gallagher**

**Liverpool (0) 1**
Scales (71)
James, Jones, Bjornebye, Scales, Ruddock, Babb, Thomas, McManaman, Rush, Barnes, Fowler.
**Subs:** Walters (for Bjornebye 51), Redknapp (for Thomas 66), Stensgaard not used.

**Queens Park Rangers (1) 1**
Gallen (5)
Roberts, Bardsley, Wilson, McDonald, Impey, Holloway, Barker, Brevett, Maddix, Gallen, Ferdinand.
**Subs:** Yates, Sinclair and Dykstra not used.

| Pos | P | W | D | L | F | Ag | Pts |
|---|---|---|---|---|---|---|---|
| **4** | **27** | **13** | **9** | **5** | **46** | **22** | **48** |

Date: **February 25th, 1995**
Venue: **Hillsborough 31,964**
Tournament: **Carling Premiership**
Referee: **David Ellery**

**Sheffield Wednesday (1) 1**
Bart Williams (14)
Pressman, Atherton, Nolan, Petrescu, Walker, Hyde, Waddle, Sinton, Bart Williams, Bright, Whittingham.
**Subs:** Sheridan (for Waddle 45), Watson (for Petrescu 74), Woods not used.

**Liverpool (1) 2**
Barnes (42), McManaman (57)
James, Jones, Bjornebye, Scales, Babb, Walters, Redknapp, Thomas, McManaman, Barnes, Fowler,.
**Subs:** Matteo (for Walters 81), Clough and Warner not used.

| Pos | P | W | D | L | F | Ag | Pts |
|---|---|---|---|---|---|---|---|
| **4** | **28** | **14** | **9** | **5** | **48** | **23** | **51** |

Date: **March 4th, 1995**
Venue: **Anfield 39,300**
Tournament: **Carling Premiership**
Referee: **Peter Jones**

**Liverpool (0) 2**
Fowler (57), Rush (63)
James, Jones, Scales, Ruddock, Babb, Walters, Redknapp, McManaman, Rush, Barnes, Fowler.
**Subs:** Thomas (for Walters 76), Molby and Warner not used.

**Newcastle (0) 0**
Srnicek, Hottiger, Berisford, Howey, Peacock, Venison, Fox, Lee, Beardsley, Gillespie, Kitson.
**Subs:** Bracewell (for Fox 83), Watson (for Beardsley 45), Hooper not used.

| Pos | P | W | D | L | F | Ag | Pts |
|---|---|---|---|---|---|---|---|
| **4** | **29** | **15** | **9** | **5** | **50** | **23** | **54** |

Date: **March 14th, 1995**
Venue: **Anfield 27,183**
Tournament: **Carling Premiership**
Referee: **Mike Reed**

**Liverpool (0) 2**
Molby pen (77), Burrows og (90)
James, Jones, Bjornebye, Scales, Ruddock, Molby, Redknapp, Thomas, McManaman, Rush, Fowler.
**Subs:** Walters (for Bjornebye 62), Wright and Warner not used.

**Coventry City (2) 3**
Ndlovu (21), pen (35, 85)
Gould, Borrows, Burrows, Rennie, Pickering, Boland, Cook, Marsh, Richardson, Ndlovu, Dublin.
**Subs:** Pressley, Williams, Ogrizovic not used.

| Pos | P | W | D | L | F | Ag | Pts |
|---|---|---|---|---|---|---|---|
| **4** | **30** | **15** | **9** | **6** | **52** | **26** | **54** |

Date: **March 19th, 1995**
Venue: **Anfield 38,906**
Tournament: **Carling Premiership**
Referee: **Gerald Ashby**

**Liverpool (1) 2**
Redknapp (24), Bruce og (85)
James, Scales, Bjornebye, Wright, Ruddock, Babb, Redknapp, McManaman, Rush, Barnes, Fowler.
**Subs:** Walters (for Rush 87), Thomas (for Barnes 61), Warner not used.

**Manchester United (0) 0**
Schmeichel, Sharpe, Irwin, Bruce, Pallister, Ince, McClair, Keane, Kanchelskis, Giggs, Hughes.
**Subs:** Cole (for Sharpe 45), Butt (for Keane 83), Pilkington not used.

| Pos | P | W | D | L | F | Ag | Pts |
|---|---|---|---|---|---|---|---|
| **4** | **31** | **16** | **9** | **6** | **54** | **26** | **57** |

Date: **March 22nd, 1995**
Venue: **White Hart Lane 31,988**
Tournament: **Carling Premiership**
Referee: **Paul Danson**

**Tottenham Hotspur (0) 0**
Walker, Austin, Edinburgh, Nethercott, Mabbutt, Barmby, Howells, Anderton, Rosenthal, Sheringham, Klinsmann.
**Subs:** Kerslake (for Nethercott 87), Caskey and Thorsvedt not used.

**Liverpool (0) 0**
James, Jones, Bjornebye, Scales, Ruddock, Babb, Redknapp, McManaman, Thomas, Walters, Fowler.
**Subs:** Clough (for Walters 78), Wright and Warner not used.

| Pos | P | W | D | L | F | Ag | Pts |
|---|---|---|---|---|---|---|---|
| **5** | **32** | **16** | **10** | **6** | **54** | **26** | **58** |

Date: **April 5th, 1995**
Venue: **Anfield 29,881**
Tournament: **Carling Premiership**
Referee: **Stephen Lodge**

**Liverpool (1) 3**
Rush (28, 53), Fowler pen (70)
James, Jones, Bjornebye, Scales, Ruddock, Babb, Redknapp, McManaman, Rush, Barnes, Fowler.
**Subs:** Walters (for Bjornebye 62), Thomas and Chamberlain not used.

**Southampton (1) 1**
Hall (14)
Grobbelaar, Dodd, Charlton, Hall, Widdrington, Le Tissier, Magilton, Maddison, Heaney, Watson, Shipperley.
**Subs:** Tisdale (for Heaney 60), Allen and Beasant not used.

| Pos | P | W | D | L | F | Ag | Pts |
|---|---|---|---|---|---|---|---|
| **5** | **33** | **17** | **10** | **6** | **57** | **27** | **61** |

Date: **April 9th, 1995**
Venue: **Anfield 37,454**
Tournament: **Carling Premiership**
Referee: **Keith Burge**

**Liverpool (0) 0**
James, Jones, Babb, Scales, Ruddock, Walters, Redknapp, McManaman, Rush, Barnes, Fowler.
**Subs:** Kennedy (for Walters 71), Thomas and Chamberlain not used.

**Leeds United (1) 1**
Deane (29)
Lukic, Kelly, Dorigo, Wetherall, Pemberton, Palmer, McAllister, Speed, Wallace, Deane, Yeboah.
**Subs:** Worthington, Whelan and Beeney not used.

| Pos | P | W | D | L | F | Ag | Pts |
|---|---|---|---|---|---|---|---|
| **5** | **34** | **17** | **10** | **7** | **57** | **28** | **61** |

Date: **April 12th, 1995**
Venue: **Highbury 38,036**
Tournament: **Carling Premiership**
Referee: **Martin Bodenham**

**Arsenal (0) 0**
Seaman, Keown, Winterburn, Adams, Bould, Helder, Schwarz, Hillier, McGoldrick, Wright, Merson.
**Subs:** Hartson (for Helder 71), Parlour (for Merson 89), Bartram not used.

**Liverpool (1) 1**
Fowler (90)
James, Jones, Babb, Scales, Ruddock, Redknapp, Thomas, McManaman, Kennedy, Barnes, Fowler.
**Subs:** Wright (for Jones 45), Walters (for Scales 57), Chamberlain not used.

| Pos | P | W | D | L | F | Ag | Pts |
|---|---|---|---|---|---|---|---|
| **5** | **35** | **18** | **10** | **7** | **58** | **28** | **64** |

Date: **April 14th, 1995**
Venue: **Maine Road 27,055**
Tournament: **Carling Premiership**
Referee: **Joe Worrall**

**Manchester City (1) 2**
Summerbee (18), Gaudino (71)
Coton, Edgehill, Phelan, Foster, Curle, Gaudino, Summerbee, Walsh, Flitcroft, Quinn, Rosler.
**Subs:** Beagrie (for Walsh 69), Kernaghan (for Phelan 60), Burridge not used.

**Liverpool (1) 1**
McManaman (21)
James, Thomas, Babb, Wright, Ruddock, Redknapp, McManaman, Kennedy, Barnes, Rush, Fowler,.
**Subs:** Matteo (for McManaman 73), Clough (for Matteo 81), Chamberlain not used.

| Pos | P | W | D | L | F | Ag | Pts |
|---|---|---|---|---|---|---|---|
| **5** | **36** | **18** | **10** | **8** | **59** | **30** | **64** |

Date: **April 17th, 1995**
Venue: **Anfield 36,012**
Tournament: **Carling Premiership**
Referee: **Graham Poll**

**Liverpool (0) 2**
Fowler (75), Rush (80)
James, Thomas, Harkness, Wright, Ruddock, Redknapp, McManaman, Kennedy, Rush, Barnes, Fowler.
**Subs:** Clough (for McManaman 81), Stewart and Chamberlain not used.

**Leicester City (0) 0**
Poole, Grayson, Whitlow, Willis, Hill, Blake, Draper, Carey, Parker, Robins, Roberts.
**Subs:** Lawrence (for Blake 73), Lowe and Ward not used.

| Pos | P | W | D | L | F | Ag | Pts |
|---|---|---|---|---|---|---|---|
| **4** | **37** | **19** | **10** | **8** | **61** | **30** | **67** |

Date: **April 29th, 1995**
Venue: **Carrow Road 21,843**
Tournament: **Carling Premiership**
Referee: **Brian Hill**

**Norwich City (1) 1**
Ullathorne (15)
Marshall, Bradshaw, Sutch, Bowen, Newsome, Polston, Crook, Milligan, Ullathorne, Ward, Akimbayi.
**Subs:** Adams (for Ullathorne 79), Cureton (for Bradshaw 75), Rhodes not used.

**Liverpool (1) 2**
Harkness (7), Rush (84)
James, Thomas, Harkness, Babb, Wright, Scales, Redknapp, McManaman, Barnes, Rush, Fowler.
**Subs:** Clough (for Barnes 73), Walters (for Fowler 80), Warner not used.

| Pos | P | W | D | L | F | Ag | Pts |
|---|---|---|---|---|---|---|---|
| **4** | **38** | **20** | **10** | **8** | **63** | **31** | **70** |

Date: **May 2nd, 1995**
Venue: **Selhurst Park 12,041**
Tournament: **Carling Premiership**
Referee: **Terry Holbrook**

**Wimbledon (0) 0**
Sullivan, Cunningham, Barton, Thorn, Reeves, Kimble, Jones, Elkins, Gayle, Perry, Goodman,.
**Subs:** Ekoku (for Goodman 74), Fear (for Gayle 89), Segers not used.

**Liverpool (0) 0**
James, Thomas, Harkness, Scales, Ruddock, Walters, Redknapp, McManaman, Barnes, Rush, Fowler.
**Subs:** Matteo (for Ruddock 64), Clough and Warner not used.

| Pos | P | W | D | L | F | Ag | Pts |
|---|---|---|---|---|---|---|---|
| **4** | **39** | **20** | **11** | **8** | **63** | **31** | **71** |

Date: **May 6th, 1995**
Venue: **Villa Park 40,184**
Tournament: **Carling Premiership**
Referee: **Robbie Hart**

**Aston Villa (2) 2**
Yorke (25, 36)
Bosnich, Charles, Wright, Ehiogu, McGrath, Teale, Staunton, Townsend, Taylor, Yorke, Saunders.
**Subs:** Fenton (for Staunton 75), Johnson and Spink not used.

**Liverpool (0) 0**
James, Thomas, Wright, Scales, Harkness, Walters, Redknapp, McManaman, Barnes, Rush, Fowler.
**Subs:** Clough (for Rush 64), Matteo (for Walters 75), Warner not used.

| Pos | P | W | D | L | F | Ag | Pts |
|---|---|---|---|---|---|---|---|
| **4** | **40** | **20** | **11** | **9** | **63** | **33** | **71** |

Date: **May 10th, 1995**
Venue: **Upton Park 22,246**
Tournament: **Carling Premiership**
Referee: **Paul Durkin**

**West Ham United (1) 3**
Holmes (29), Hutchison (60, 61)
Miklosko, Breacker, Dicks, Potts, Rieper, Hughes, Bishop, Moncur, Holmes, Hutchison, Morley.
**Subs:** Webster (for Dicks 13), Allen and Sealey not used.

**Liverpool (0) 0**
James, Thomas, Babb, Scales, Harkness, Redknapp, McManaman, Matteo, Barnes, Clough, Fowler.
**Subs:** Walters (for Fowler 71), Kennedy (for Matteo 61), Warner not used.

| Pos | P | W | D | L | F | Ag | Pts |
|---|---|---|---|---|---|---|---|
| **5** | **41** | **20** | **11** | **10** | **63** | **36** | **71** |

Date: **May 14th, 1995**
Venue: **Anfield 40,014**
Tournament: **Carling Premiership**
Referee: **David Elleray**

**Liverpool (0) 2**
Barnes (64), Redknapp (90)
James, Thomas, Babb, Scales, Harkness, Redknapp, McManaman, Kennedy, Barnes, Clough and Fowler.
**Subs:** Matteo (for Scales 82), Walters, Warner not used

**Blackburn Rovers (1) 1**
Shearer (20)
Flowers, Berg, Kenna, Hendry, Pearce, Sherwood, Le Saux, Batty, Ripley, Sutton, Shearer
**Subs:** Newell, Slater, Mimms not used.

| Pos | P | W | D | L | F | Ag | Pts |
|---|---|---|---|---|---|---|---|
| **4** | **42** | **21** | **11** | **10** | **65** | **37** | **74** |